Towards Salvaging Humanity
(Selected Speeches)

Ahsan Academy of Research

(Springs, South Africa)

Towards Salvaging Humanity
(Selected Speeches)

by

Sayyid Abul Hasan Ali Nadwi

Edited by

Abdul Kader Choughley

Tawasul International

Centre for Publishing, Research and Dialogue

First Published 2023
Second Edition 2024
ISBN: 9781445791715

Ahsan Academy of Research
(Springs, South Africa)

Tawasul International
Centre for Publishing, Research and Dialogue
(Rome, Italy)

CONTENTS

Preface

Payām i - Insaniyāt (Message for Humanity)

The origins of the *Payām* movement go back to the early 1950s when, in the wake of growing attacks on Muslims by Hindu extremist groups, Shaykh Abul Hasan Ali Nadwi began addressing joint Hindu-Muslim public rallies, calling for communal harmony and peace. In the course of his interaction with Hindus in various parts of India he discovered that many of them had doubts and misunderstanding about Islam, which further widened the gulf between them. This led him, in 1974, to formally launch *Payām i - Insāniyat.*

The activities of *Payām* consisted, mainly, in organising public rallies addressed by Shaykh Nadwi, his deputy Shaykh Abdul Karim Parikh of Nagpur, as well as other Muslim and Hindu leaders. It also was responsible for publishing literature in various languages on communal harmony, largely from the writings of Shaykh Nadwi. His speeches generally focused on moral values, communal hatred, violence and oppression of marginalised groups, social vices and corruption in public life. He, however, strongly believed that India could progress only in a climate of peace, free from communal violence. For Muslims, this message was clear: they were enjoined by Islam to build friendly relations with other faith communities rather than alienating them.

According to Shaykh Nadwi, the essence of *Payām* was to exemplify the teachings of Islam through Muslim interaction with others. Not only was this their religious duty, it was also imperative if they were to live in security and peace as a minority group.

In advocating peace with others Muslims, Shaykh Nadwi insisted, would not be betraying their religion. Rather, he pointed out, Islam is clear that human beings, irrespective of religion, race, caste and class, are "the most precious" of Allah's creation, and an "expression of Divine mercy." This being the case, Muslims should strive for peace and must also raise their voices against all forms of oppression. In this way, they would show others that they are an integral segment of the country rather than a burden. But peace, he pointed out, could not be achieved if one community sought to impose its beliefs or culture on the others.

As much as religious tolerance had the potential to promote communal harmony, Shaykh Nadwi also believed that democracy and secularism were mechanisms through which *Payām* could achieve its aims.

The core message of the movement was based on unconditional love for humanity. Shaykh Nadwi observed:

- The excellence of man lies in his love and mercy for others: one person is pricked with a thorn but another feels the pain. Man is gifted with tears which fall from his eyes when he sees a widow's head uncovered in helplessness, a poor man's kitchen unlit and a sick man in distress.

- According to Shaykh Nadwi, religion fosters faith and love for the Creator in the hearts and removes deception from the eyes. It was the work of Messengers to remove the curtain of darkness from the eyes and bring peace and tranquility to the hearts. He observed:

- We tell Muslims that you have devalued the message and work of Messengers. You are guilty of being negligent. You have abandoned the treasure and have become an agent of the greedy people of the world. You have become a mere bargainer and developed a mentality of a selfish businessman. You were not supposed to be a mere trader. You had come here as a *dāʻi* (one who invites to Islam) but you forgot your position and purpose for which you had come.

- Political parties and other outfits, instead of fighting for power and control, should strive to mend the broken structure of humanity. Likewise, they should refrain from only working for their own interests and of their own friends and relatives. Overall, they should work for the welfare of the entire mankind. Without this reform, no one can achieve peace and success.

Reflections on *Payām*

The subcontinent had witnessed over the centuries a plethora of religious activities that focused on the sanctity of human life, quest for righteous living, social upliftment, and most importantly, the interiorisation of spirituality. Alongside the evolution of Indo-Islamic culture, there was a blending of religio-mystical traits resulting from the convergence of faiths in the subcontinent. Framed from the lens of a cosmopolitan outlook, the rich tapestry of an evolving nation woven into the universal expression of love, compassion and brotherhood became more pronounced. These forms may have differed in the multicultural nation but the imprint was permanent and significant. And it was in the subcontinent that the *insāniyat* (humanity) theme was raised and nurtured on indigenous soil.

Muslim-Hindu co-existence existed from the early years of Muslim rule. It was, however, the British imperialist policies that caused a rift between the two communities. It was evident that the simmering tensions that surfaced from the late nineteenth century were politically motivated. In response to these rising tensions, the principles of secularism and non-violence were enshrined in the Constitution after the Partition in 1947 to safeguard the rights of its citizens. These constitutionally protective measures, however, did not deter Hindu extremists from accusing Muslims of supporting the nascent Pakistan cause. In the years that followed communal tensions flared up with a vengeance: Muslims were victims of a deliberate campaign by *Hindutva* (Hindu extremism) to obliterate their collective Islamic identity. Thousands of lives were lost during the communal riots, and in their aftermath, the slogan of universal peace turned into a fragile truce negotiated by influential leaders of both communities.

The *Payām* movement must be understood in the context of the volatile situations existing in the country. Shaykh Nadwi's call had a two-fold purpose: first, to create a climate of mutual harmony so that faith-based communities might not harbour suspicions on the basis of patriotic loyalty. In this instance, Muslims were on the receiving end of hostility largely on account of ignorance by other communities. They were held culpable for the perceived excesses against the Hindu majority by past Muslim rulers. More perturbing was the notion that Muslims of India wholeheartedly supported the Pakistan state.

Second, Shaykh Nadwi believed that the reconstruction of the Indian society was only possible if the process of moral regeneration was set into motion. This approach was in response to the scourge of corruption, cronyism, nepotism and other vices that had sapped the dynamism of a great country. Instead, political parties and the bureaucratic system worked in cahoots to deepen the social inequality that was rampant over the decades. In this strain, Shaykh Nadwi's *Payām* was unequivocal in its declaration that communities would inevitably live in isolation and tear apart the fabric of a stable society. Needless to add, moral anarchy, social greed and political instability delinked the citizens from constructive ideals. As a result, mutual respect, empathy and humanitarian initiatives became hollow expressions that impeded the implementation of universal values. In keeping with the tradition of Nizām al-Din Awliyā, the great saint of Delhi, Shaykh Nadwi echoed a similar sentiment:

Thorns spread on the pathway will he a thorny issue. Plant flowers instead so that the pathway may he lush with flowers and flowers only.

On the contrary, if moral vices eroded the collective life and outlook of society then divine punishment was inevitable. Shaykh Nadwi was forthright in this regard:

I am a man of religious convictions. My study of history tells me that sins and wrongdoings invite the wrath of Allah in the form of natural calamities.

Allah warns us through these disasters. He tells us that He has greater power to destroy us than we have. When I hear of any cruelty and oppression, I shudder at the thought of divine punishment visiting people. I make no exception for anybody in this matter. Whenever acts of savagery and brutality occur, Allah's punishment is sure to visit upon the wrongdoers in a way unimaginable and unpredictable by the most learned astrologer. The problems relating to economic and social reconstruction get complicated, law and order situation deteriorates, administrative apparatus becomes loose and ineffective, intellectual and political leadership is rendered incapable of solving myriad issues facing the country which becomes weak internally and loses prestige in the international forums.

Shaykh Nadwi stressed on the awakening of the human spirit, as is evident from his speech on 2 December 1990:

- What has sustained man throughout, from the earliest phase of history is that good persons have never lost faith in fellow human beings. They did not dismiss others as incorrigible animals or terminally ill patients. They did not harbour revulsion towards them. Nor did they deny their rights to existence.

- The light of humanity can always be kindled. It survives under all hostile conditions. History testifies that Messengers of Allah always protected this light. They bore personal hardships, hunger, roamed in forests and deserts in inclement weather for serving humanity. No discomfort demoralised them or dissuaded them from their noble mission. What lay behind their inexhaustible energy and their ceaseless efforts was their belief that man is Nature's masterpiece.

The need for divine guidance is articulated by Shaykh Nadwi:

- Messengers of Allah placed restraint on desires and urged man to be moderate in gratifying his desires. Far from stoking base desires they infused into man a strong desire for pleasing Allah and developing sympathy for fellow human beings.

We are keen on instilling the above quest for truth. Life does not stand for eating or drinking. Man should not lead a materialistic or animal life. We wish to infuse a new thirst which may sound novel today. However, our message is the one which was brought by all Messengers to their respective communities. The same message was most forcefully and clearly presented by Prophet Muhammad (peace be upon him) as the final word. This truth should be reiterated everywhere. Man is attracted only to his animal instincts, ignoring his true self. Mankind is in serious loss. We raise the call to truth with which the world might be unfamiliar. Yet we have not despaired of mankind. Man is gifted with conscience which is not dead. It is only clouded. Once it is cleansed of pollution, man is likely to greet truth and develop faith.

In order to avoid the subtle trappings of the unity of religions approach, Shaykh Nadwi reminded his audience that divine guidance serves as a common platform to articulate the concerns of the Indian society. In sum, *Payām* was a pioneering movement with no formal structures and yet had a sobering impact on society. By and large, Shaykh Nadwi generally spoke at these meetings to ensure that there was no semblance of syncretic faiths. More often than not, speakers were inclined to overstep the boundaries of *Payām* that inadvertently created a climate for religious debates. In Shaykh Nadwi's estimation, these were counterproductive to the goals set out by him for establishing the movement.

Payām had a considerable impact on changing the mindset of many citizens belonging to different faiths in the country. It fervently believed in the unity of mankind which effectively had the potential to bring about lasting peace not only in India but across the world. In Shaykh Nadwi's view, the malaise affecting mankind was a global phenomenon. Therefore, the remedy derived from the divine sources was clear and consistent.

Following Shaykh Nadwi's demise in 1999, this noble effort continued under the visionary leadership of Sayyid Bilal Abdul Hayy Hasani. Apart from disseminating *Payām*'s message through public speeches, its outreach program has also succeeded in creating a climate of social cohesion. In contrast to political organisations advocating agitational politics and vested communal interest, *Payām* has consistently steered clear of politics as envisioned by its founder, Shaykh Nadwi. Rather, it works on the innate goodness of the human spirit and the need for moral regeneration.

In recent times the disdain for universal values has become a painful reality. Base desire or lust divides humanity into fragmented units with the result that dignity is lost to brutality. The spectre of mob lynching, xenophobic attacks and gender-based violence is a manifestation of mankind degenerating at an alarming level. It is almost a daily experience that desensitises our compassionate disposition. To counter these anti-humanity tendencies, the need to establish movements like *Payām* cannot be overemphasised.

<h1 style="text-align:center">Chapter 1</h1>

<h2 style="text-align:center">The Nightmare of Our Life[1]</h2>

What can boost man's morale most?

The Chair and Dear Listeners!

It is a matter of great pleasure and honour for me to address you in this historic city. It represents the confluence of not only rivers but also of various movements. Some significant movements which influenced the whole country were set in motion in this city. Once again, this city has provided even internationally acclaimed political leaders and administrators to both our state and country.

What boosts one's morale most is his realisation that he is trusted by someone, and is not distrusted. Confidence should be reposed in him. Likewise, he should be heard properly. His concerns, especially his misery should be addressed. Rather, efforts should be made to share his sorrow. Without such conduct, those gifted with tender feelings, conscience and sensitive heart will feel upset. On the contrary, this world will be reduced into a big market with two parties: a) a seller and b) a customer. Needless to add, it will not be a joyful world to live in. For there will be nothing worthwhile. If only the rich are reckoned as the most fortunate persons, all values will lose their meaning and relevance.

To err is not unnatural for man

To err does not run counter to man's nature. This truism is recognised by those well-grounded in religion, moral philosophy, history, psychology, and ethics. Lapses are an asset for man. Without lapses there is no essential difference between man and an inanimate stone. For the latter cannot err. By the same token, it cannot improve itself either. Man is liable to committing many lapses. However, he has the ability to confess his lapses and to resolve not to do these in future. He learns lessons from his mistakes. It is

---

[1] In view of the deteriorating moral conditions and violation of values in the country, Nadwi had launched *Payām i-Insāniyat* (Message for Humanity) on 28- 30 December 1974 in Allahabad. The speech may be considered as the inaugural address of the *Payām* movement.

not bad in itself to err. However, the inability to learn from mistakes is man's tragedy.

It is not outrageous that man errs or indulges in sins. Had it not been so, there was no need or relevance of moral teachers, and Messengers of Allah. It would not have entailed any test or trial. Man would then have no struggle to face. The real joy of life consists in facing the ordeal between good and evil and in countering the effects of evil. One feels gratified as he attains self-development. All the joys in life, including the conflict amid various forces and new vistas are owing to the diversity in man's life. One is pitted against conflicting ideas and varying claims. There is always a battle between opposing ideas and emotions. Man errs and then concedes his mistake. He loses something and then strives to recover his loss. Without this loss and gain, life is stripped of its charms. As one gets something he enjoys it. It is pointless to take man to task for his errors. For committing errors is common to everyone, including you and me in an equal degree. It would be futile to expect man to turn into an angel. This was not expected even by Messengers of Allah. Nor had they demanded this of man. Man cannot be transformed into an inanimate object like a stone. There is a vast difference between a stone and an angel. I am fully familiar with this distinction. Yet, what is common to both is that neither of them errs. Man's virtue and strength lie in his proneness to err. And he commits many mistakes. However, he realises his mistakes and tries to overcome these. At times, he admits his mistakes, which enhance his prestige. His erring does not lower his prestige or honour.

Joys of Life

The joy of life consists in mutual trust and understanding so that we may listen to one another. If we distrust one another, it would make our life horrible. We should not prejudge others and attribute motives to them.

Since this gathering comprises many highly educated persons, my optimism has grown. I have now greater confidence in that so many people have turned up with good intentions, looking forward to listen to something useful.

Our story

This story may be elaborated or abridged. It is not some ancient story. Nor is it specific to any particular nation or country. Rather it is our own story. God has been immensely kind to us in having bestowed upon us numerous bounties and has been providing us with so much. He has showered His favours on us and granted us the best possible opportunities and means. All the treasures of the world lie at our disposal. He has favoured us with a vast country which is rich in natural resources. Moreover, it boasts of a glorious history. Our country, India is a world unto itself, though in geographical terms it is only a country. It is nothing short of a continent. One finds it hard to traverse across its vast territory. If any of you has been to south India, he is bound to bear out its huge size.

Some of you must have visited Europe. I have been there a few times for academic purposes. Some of the European countries are so small that one does not even realise that he has already crossed one and entered another. In comparison, ours is like a continent. One gets tired of traveling its long distances even by fast moving trains. At times, one spends a couple of days and nights while traveling yet he does not cover the distance to his destination.

God has gifted us a big country, populated by millions of people. Our countrymen have a rich legacy of culture, literature and traditions. We are fortunate to have plenty of natural resources. Indians are kind-hearted by nature. They have a genuine interest in truth and profess and practice justice. The quest for God has been pursued here in all times. Not only have Indians discovered the higher truths, they have transmitted these to others as well, including people abroad.

We inherited this country at a time when the world was steeped in materialism. Many countries experimented but these were not by and large successful. Their plans did not materialize. As a result, mankind was lost in a morass.

A Tragedy

Educated people know it well that it is not a child's play to assume the leadership of the world and to be at the helm of affairs. Intense efforts are called for it, along with true mettle. It is tragic that the leadership of the world has gone into the hands of those who do not recognize God. Nor do they have any respect for humanity. Their only objectives are political hegemony, enslaving other nations of the world, establishing their control over more and more countries, exploitation of their subjects, monopolizing and exploiting their resources and using these for conquering neighboring countries. They are devoted only to subduing others.

The dilemma of Europe is that it has small countries, with very limited resources. There has been a long history of rivalry among German, French and English people. They were therefore compelled to extend their rule and capture the world market, monopolize resources and means and thus assert their supremacy. This was the mindset of landlords and feudal lords which now grips these nations. The French were bent on knocking out the Germans by way of having their colonies across the world. They targeted the illiterate black Africans and other so-called uncivilised people. They enslaved them in order to prove to the Germans that they are a mighty force. Same holds true of the British's conduct.

It was a colossal tragedy for mankind that the European leadership was not imbued with humane values[2]. It failed to respect those who deserved it. Nor did it note that God has boundless love for His servants.

Sincerity and Love are Powerful Forces

We recognize Prophet Jesus (peace be upon him) as Allah's Messenger. He instructed mankind in love and sympathy for all human beings and God-consciousness. However, Europe imbibed this message little. They accepted Christianity as a matter of pride yet they did not draw fully upon his teachings. On account of the European leadership the whole mankind has landed into serious troubles. There is an economic rat race, full of competition in which everyone strives to outpace others. The Oriental and Asian nations, blessed with divine faith, should have exercised their sway over mankind. They should have demonstrated a perfect example of their sincerity, asserting that man's issues cannot be resolved only by intelligence and science and technology. Rather, these are solved by mutual love and sincerity. Messengers of Allah are acclaimed even today, some thousands of years after their demise. People have overflowing love for them and hold them in esteem. The two major calendars, solar and lunar, are in commemoration of the two great prophets. The entire world follows these calendars. It is reflective of their abiding imprint on human life and culture.

The Messengers annexed their high position by dint of their sincerity. We too, should have displayed an example of utmost sincerity. We could show how with little resources much can be achieved. We should have asserted the power and spell of love. Thus, we would have affirmed something which is rare and for which everyone yearns. We do not lack talent, intelligence, industry, and science and technology. However, we are devoid of mutual love and sincerity.

---

[2] For a detailed discussion on the pervasive influence of colonialism, see Nadwi, *Western Civilisation, Islam and Muslims* (Lucknow, 1974).

Chapter 1

The Nightmare of Our Life

All-encompassing Distrust

Every action of ours today is prompted by some motive. The philosophy behind election is based wholly on motives. Propelled by our selfish interests we resort to pleading, faltering, striving and making sweet promises. Today no one behaves selflessly towards others. We are chained to our habits and are governed by our experience. Even if one acts selflessly, others discover motives. We have grown so cynical that we do not trust anyone. We believe that everyone has some selfish motive behind his actions. Even some countries are plagued by this distrust. Everyone has to be on his guard, as they do not trust one another. Man is deemed as utterly unreliable and hence the all-encompassing distrust. One does not repose confidence even in his real brother. Our country is under the same spell as we have grown sceptic. We do not honestly express what we feel. It is a hell-like experience if one is unable to say what he wants.

My dear brethren!

We must reflect on serious issues haunting our life. Presently some persons display discontent only on political grounds. I do not reject politics altogether in that it is an important part of our life. It is a reality that a political movement helped achieve the freedom of our country. This town, Allahabad played a key role in this Freedom movement. We all are thus indebted in varying degrees to politics. However, there is much which is above and beyond politics.

The Terminal Stage of the Decline of Humanity

Once an epidemic breaks out, afflicting the heart and mind, its only remedy is sincere sympathy which has been bequeathed to us by Messengers of Allah. They had appeared on the scene in an era vitiated by mutual distrust. People then suffered from their inside which is the terminal stage of the decline of humanity. If one's body is diseased, it can be cured. However, if one's soul is affected by distrust, despondency, pessimism and selfishness, this represents a diseased state of mind and soul. This is akin to the throes of death. As one loses faith in mankind, in his community and in the reform of his country, and in everyone, he turns grossly self-centred. For he then thinks only of his interest, as he stops caring about his country, believing that his country is beyond redemption.

Likewise, he awaits its destruction in the near future. Once this mindset develops, it becomes very hard to salvage.

Dangerous Mindset

What we fear most is that everyone thinks that the real issue hurting our country inhabited by millions of people cannot be solved. Any effort in this direction amounts to wasting time and energy in this useless pursuit. This betrays an alarming mindset. Though people do not say it in so many words, they have turned cynical. They are obsessed with grabbing as many benefits as possible. Everyone is given to unfair means owing the ailments around us and the wrong direction taken by our country.

Here is an example. If we read this news report that an airplane, God forbid, crashed in a farm and the local villagers robbed the victims of their valuables and ran away with all that they could grab, we will feel revulsion towards this heinous misdeed. We will curse those callous persons and take them as worse than beasts. For they acted thus in such circumstances. They should have rescued the victims, saved their lives, offered them water and expressed sympathy with them. On the contrary, they brazenly looted them.

You are bound to condemn this incident and curse the culprits, saying that such insensitive persons will incur God's wrath.

The Present scenario of Our Country

Our country at present is like that crashed airplane, of which the passengers are mercilessly robbed by an insensitive crowd.

Why do you not feel revulsion at this state of affairs? Our fate is inextricably linked with our country. If this boat sinks, all of us will drown. No one will be spared, including the pious and the devout or scholars. All inside the boat will be afflicted. Once the boat sinks, no one will ensure a safe passage for the pious. Nor will there be any divine intervention for rescuing the noble persons. Such salvaging is improbable and discordant with reason, experience and history. Everyone on board will drown.

Given this, I ask you as to why you take this country like that crashed airplane? We are already on the brink of that stage. Do we await further downfall? What is the scenario in our country? All of us are engrossed in getting as much as we can for our own benefit. Corruption, laziness at work, taking advantage of others, insisting on our due and depriving others of their due are rife. We are not fair towards others.

No one of us feels any concern for fellow citizens. Nor do we have any sympathy or human link with them. We all are Indians, inhabiting the same

The Nightmare of Our Life

country yet we do not feel like helping anyone. We think that we are on a sinking ship and hence our frantic effort to get as much as we can. We are keen on appropriating everything for ourselves. This is a very grave situation and a diseased mind. Nothing can be salvaged in such a scenario.

Awakening of Conscience along with Freedom

It was all right to secure the Freedom of our country. Rather, we should have invested ten times more in this cause. Those who strove for this deserve all credit not only in Indian history but in world history. For they performed a sacred duty. I must nonetheless add that Freedom was no doubt an important cause. However, we should have liberated people as well. People are in bondage of various kinds. A foreign power may rule and hold us in bondage. It may establish its agencies, administration and system and reap benefits. However, man may be enslaved in many ways. His base desires, love of oppression, apathy to injustice, dishonesty, Mammon worship, disrespect for humanity and many other vices may reign supreme over him.

It was a noble effort to liberate the country. It should have of course received top priority. Equally important, however, it was to awaken our countrymen's conscience. The liberation of body alone does not suffice. This truth has now become manifest, as many nations have attained Freedom. Yet their conscience is still a slave. Same applies to us. We are still enslaved by the British culture, worldview and diplomacy[3].

Bondage of Conscience hurts more

Not only foreigners, the very local people also commit injustice. This is our folly that we are very sensitive to the injustice by foreigners. However, we use pleasant labels and pretexts for the injustice which we do. We do not even consider it as injustice.

We are by now used to injustice. Rather, we love it, as it has permeated our heart and mind. It is our second nature. Swayed by the love of money we abandon our brothers, parents and children. Wealth is our only concern. This is what has landed us, our country and everyone into trouble. If you do not misconstrue me, this bondage of conscience is worse than foreign

---

[3] Nadwi gives a detailed account about the patriotic spirit behind the Freedom struggle of the Indian subcontinent against the entrenched British rule. See Nadwi, *Muslims in India* (Lucknow, 1976), 105-23.

rule. We have secured our Freedom, which was our duty. We, however, neglected the following important duties of awakening Indians' conscience, and purifying them of sins and love of wealth.

Injustice to be condemned in all its forms

If an Indian resorts to injustice, he is no less evil than a German, French or Englishman. If you do not concur with this, I will not support you. I will insist on saying that injustice is to be condemned, no matter who commits it. The British were unjust yet they administered everything well, better than we do now. I know that it is a harsh statement which even my conscience resents. Yet I will reiterate it. There was better law and order then. One could travel safely, not fearing any crime. Today, train robbery is fairly common, as is evident from news reports. Deadly insects have bred among us. The British were no doubt barbaric. However, they lived in Civil Lines, in their palatial houses, lost in the memory of their home and like homing pigeons they returned to London in every vacation. However, our own criminals are with us all the time. We are no longer safe. Love of wealth and sins has crept into our heart and mind. We have no respect for human beings. We are interested only in our gains and do not care about anyone.

Widespread Corruption and Maladministration in our country

Our state offices, courts, railway stations, post offices - in short, all public service offices are in a mess. During the British period these very departments were known for their efficiency and punctuality. To my good fortune, I receive many letters daily. I send letters as well and hence have my first-hand experience. I travel a lot by train. I do not know how much I have to travel more. My travel extends to overseas as well. In the light of my extensive experience, I tell you that without bribery you cannot get anything done.

The government has provided all sorts of facilities. However, people are obsessed with only getting more and more, and that too unlawfully. They have no scruples in cheating their own countrymen.

If you want to book a seat in a train, you are told that no seat is available, as all have already been allotted. However, on entering the train you see empty seats in both first and second- class compartments. An illegal business flourishes there. It is a bitter truth and in relating it I find it detestable.

What is the condition of our country now? Who stops us from doing while we enjoy freedom? Is all this because of illiteracy? I am not so credulous to buy this story. I keep telling my Arab friends that our country has so many universities which they cannot even imagine.

Lack of any constructive effort

Do you think that all problems are owing to the lack of resources? The real reason is the lack of any roadmap for constructive activities. Had we devoted even a little of the energy which we spent on our Freedom movement, had we striven for the moral construction of our society, we would have turned into good human beings. We would have learnt values, teaching us that sin, injustice, oppression and cheating are evil. If one usurps someone's money, it is like poison, not money for the offender. It is worse than deadly animals. However, we care little about unfair means and try to amass money by any means.

Natural Way

As you plant a *neem*[4] sapling, water it and take good care of it, it will bear fruits. However, on tasting its bitter taste, if you curse that tree, and accuse it of ingratitude in returning your favours so uncharitably, no one will have any sympathy for you. For you had planted this bitter fruit tree. You should not expect to reap anything other than what you sow.

A Moral Case

I protest against having nurtured the Western culture in our country. I file this case in people's court and seek an honest judge's ruling. While standing in the honourable people's court in Allahabad, I want to file a moral case. I know that the High Court in this town has redressed the grievances of thousands of victims and restored what was due to orphans and widows. I do not think that the ambit of court is very narrow. I urge you to decide this moral case. If I do not have access to Allahabad High Court, my plea should strike a chord in your conscience and heart. You have an innate sense of justice. That is why courts are in place. In the absence of this innate human instinct, enlightenment, knowledge and efforts, these courts could not come into existence. You have created these courts. You are not brought

---

[4] The *neem* tree belongs to the mahogany family and is used for pesticidal purposes. It is also widely used as a hair and dental product.

into being by them. My case is against this corrupt philosophy of life, against the entire materialistic culture and against the present political system. I seek your ruling. You have created this vicious atmosphere and hence you cannot complain against it. Do you have a desire to rebel against the present state of affairs?

God has let you grow as a sane adult. He has informed you well the consequences of this and that action. He has ordained that soil will produce only what is sown. He waters seeds and plants grow naturally according to their characteristics. Rain and soil cannot deviate from God's laws. However, God does not compel educated, mature men to do only one type of actions.

He has granted them Free Will. Man is free to do what he wants. If one does something, he cannot resent its consequences. We will be unjustified in complaining.

A Major Lapse

We did evil deeds and did not teach any child about God's existence. We do not tell him about the ultimate death. We do not instruct him in God-man relationship. We do not impart to him at all such knowledge. This is not part of our curriculum, right from primary class up to Ph.D. and D. Litt at the University of Allahabad. We teach him such points which do not affect his ultimate end. The knowledge pursued by us is neither good nor bad for his fate. We tell nothing what may transform man's condition and turn the present world into Paradise. Without possessing such knowledge our life is no worse than Hell.

Did we tell our children, be they Muslim or Hindu, at any stage that becoming a good human being is the best thing or that this world is God's best handiwork? We do not ask them to serve and please God. We do not instruct them in love and respect for others. They too are like our parents and children. Did we advise that any money earned illegally is like fire for them? Such moral lessons were given by Messengers of Allah. Have we created a society which abhors illegal money? There have been such glorious examples of noble souls who declined kingship. They would starve, though they could have quality food and enjoy life. Yet they turned a blind eye to all the worldly charms.

Moral Decline

The moral decline has set so much in our society that as someone approaches a government office for getting his legitimate work done, he is taken as a prey rather as a mouse in their trap. They never think that he is one of them, a fellow Indian and helping him is a duty for them. They should take it as a God-send opportunity to serve a fellow human being. What is this mindset and such callousness that we consider someone in need of help as a prey to be exploited financially? They rob him of his hard-earned money in order to placate their own family members. It does not occur to them that he too, is someone's dear one, loved by his parents, who was brought up amid much hardship. He was not sent to an office for exploitation. Is he only something that produces money?

Our country and society have reached the nadir of moral decay. Yet there is no ray of hope and no organized effort for reform. This meeting organized by us, our journey and our efforts do not match the magnitude of the task at hand. However, movements arise in this very manner. As one conveys our message to others, we would grow into a big caravan.

Allahabad, the starting point of *Payām i - Insaniyāt*

We have commenced our mission at Allahabad which literally means God's town. It deserves to be the starting point of this mission inviting everyone to Godliness and respect for humanity. It is here that we should pledge to serve mankind. We do not aim at creating some new organisation. We strive only for recalling the forgotten lesson of helping mankind. We do feel that if this mission is not taken up, the future of our country will be bleak and even our freedom and safety will be in jeopardy. No cosmetic step can be taken to rescue us[5].

---

[5] *Ta'meer i - Hayāt* (Lucknow), 10-25 January 1975. The magazine is the official organ of Nadwat al -'Ulamā (hereafter Nadwah). Nadwi served as Rector of this prestigious institution from 1961-99.

Chapter 2

God Not Despaired of the Human Race[1]

God's stance on the Human Race

Friends!

I am gratified to note this large gathering. For you have assembled here for the cause of humanity and for reflecting on the issue afflicting humanity. There is no personal or political motive behind your assembling here. This has inspired me and I feel rejuvenated in my commitment. For I can now see a ray of hope about the bright future of mankind. I no longer feel dejected.

God's stance towards the human race is opposed to our own response to fellow human beings. God is not despaired of the human race. He has been still showering His bounties upon the whole universe. Nature appears optimistic about the human race. However, our conduct betrays cynicism.

A thinker is on record observing that the birth of every baby declares that God has not given up hope about the human race. Had it not been so, He would not have added anyone to the human race. He would not have caused the birth of another baby to try his luck.

Our attitude towards fellow human beings

Man is, however, after the blood of other men. He hates, exploits and oppresses them, indicating that he is sceptic about the talents and future of mankind.

This disparity between the attitude of God and man is an eye opener. Every drop of rain water declares that the Creator of this world cares about His thirsty creatures, even though they be wrongdoers. Soil is capable of producing anything, signifying that God does not think that the future of mankind is bleak. The sun shines uninterruptedly, without any pause. The moon rises regularly and blesses everyone with its light. The moonlight cools our eyes and spirit. All this is reflective of the truth that God is not despaired of mankind.

However, our own misconduct illustrates that we do not trust other human beings. We do not pay any attention to them, though they stand out as God's best creation.

---

[1] Nadwi, *Introduction: An Islam* (Lucknow, 1998), 152-55.

Man is God's best creation

God's creative wonder is at work in every object of Nature, be it a flower, bud, drop of water, blade of grass, dust particle or leaf. Each and every object represents as world unto itself. Yet man stands out as God's best creation. All objects in Nature have been created for serving mankind. This shows that he is God's favourite, the supreme creature and the alpha and omega of the entire universe.

However, our actions suggest that man is devoid of any quality. We tend to tell God otherwise. We are after our own destruction. We thus want to vindicate the angels' plea before God which He had rejected. At the time of man's creation God declared: "I am going to create a vicegerent on earth." Upon this the angels expressed their apprehension: "Will You create him as the vicegerent who will cause discord on earth and shed blood?" When God asked Adam about the name of things, he answered correctly while angels failed in this test. God had made man victorious yet we are bent on harming and destroying him[2].

Misery makes man perfect

God told the angels that man is endowed with many potentials, capacity for gaining knowledge excelling that of oceans, and overflowing love and pathos in his heart. He is invested with tender emotions. Muhammad Iqbal, a distinguished Urdu poet, audaciously states in his couplet that angels emulate man in his spiritual ecstasy, for they are confined only to the remembrance of God in a ritualistic way. He further observes that God created man with feelings and emotions. Otherwise, angels sufficed for obeying God. Angels do not share man's vast range of both tender and lofty feelings. As opposed to angels, man can lay bare before God his anguished heart. Another Urdu poet, Amir Minā'i aptly sums up this scenario saying that man may moan and cry, as another human being is hurt. For he has overflowing love and sympathy for everyone.

Man should pain at anyone's suffering. Mercy is his most outstanding asset. He should have deep love and sympathy for everyone in distress, for a

---

[2] "They (angels) said: Glory to You. We have no knowledge except what You taught us. You, only You, are All-Knowing, All-Wise." (2: 32)

God not Despaired of the Human Race

widow, a needy person and someone ill. His love for others may help him attain expiation and salvation. Angels are capable of many things. However, they do not have that fellow feeling which makes man cry over another person's misery. We cannot measure the value of that tear which is shed over someone's suffering. A sensitive person cries at night over the all-round plight of man while everyone is fast asleep.

Angels cannot fall asleep whereas man notwithstanding his desire to sleep does not go to bed on noting another person's pain. This is something far more precious than the constant wakefulness of angels.

Man's most precious asset

Man's excellence consists in his sharing someone's pain. He is prompted by love and other considerations and in so doing he disregards the distinctions of caste, colour and creed. His overflowing love transcends the labels of nationality and country. He feels and shares others' pain. The human heart is like a magnet which pulls and is pulled towards fellow human beings.

Tears of sympathy

One is devoid of everything if he does not possess such tender feelings. If a country has all the wealth of US, Russia and Middle Eastern oil reserves, yet it is not endowed with love, it will turn morally and spiritually sterile. It will not receive any divine mercy.

Man is capable of sharing others' distress, taking pity on them and feeling things around him. If he does not have such a heart, he is a stone-hearted person who has no value in the eyes of God, be he a Muslim, Hindu, Sikh or Christian. One should cry and express love, sympathy and mercy for everyone. His tearful eye may excel even a heavy rainfall.

A Callous Person

One devoid of tender feelings cannot be called a man. He should be a sensitive soul, concerned about humanity and repentant over his own lapses. Otherwise, he is like an inanimate rock.

One who does not come forward to help humanity is like a paralysed person. Likewise, one who rushes to kill another person is worse than a beast. Had man's purpose in life been to kill others, God would have endowed him with a sword, rather than hands. Similarly, if man's only goal were to hoard wealth, a safe would have been placed in his chest rather than a throbbing heart. Had man's only pursuit been to create evil, in place of his own brain, the brain of a devil would have been provided to him.

Shaykh Abdul Karim Parikh[3], who addressed you before me dwelt at length on the marvels of the human body. However, the wonders of man's innermost being surpass those of his anatomy. Man is gifted with such a sensitive heart that he shudders at the pain of someone in the East though he himself lives in the West. An instance in point is that when the captives at the battle of Badr were chained, Prophet Muhammad (peace be upon him) could not sleep at night, feeling distressed over their plight. While leading prayer, he cut it short on hearing a baby's cry so that his mother may not feel anxious. However, if one offends someone, it is very unbecoming of him.

The danger from within

God's conduct, marked by utmost love and mercy, indicates that He is not despaired of the human race. We are used to the stoppage of such essential services as water and electricity. Going by the same logic, God can also deny His favours to us. The Bhopal Municipality provides water supply to you in good faith and has been serving you. God blesses us with food and water. Each one of us is commanded to serve Him. All objects of Nature, including rain, wind, the sum and the moon and the heavens are subservient to man. God has not given us up. However, what is our conduct? Do we demonstrate any self-respect? Do we hold others dear? The truth is that all humans being Adam's children represent one single unit.

Our inhuman attitude is the most serious threat for mankind. There is no aggression from without. In the bygone eras one nation would attack another. Now the onslaught is from within i.e. of hostility towards other human beings and decline of human values. We have turned blind to the welfare of others. Let us protect our nation and country against this threat.

Lack of Ideals

I recall here the following parable recounted to me by an elderly figure of Allahabad who had recently passed away!

---

[3] Abdul Karim Parikh (d.2007) was the co-founder of the *Payām* movement. He was a close companion of Nadwi and contributed through a series of books to the *Payām* cause. His translation of the Qur'an into Urdu has been widely acclaimed for its simplicity and charm.

Chapter 2

God not Despaired of the Human Race

A wedding procession was passing in its full splendour, accompanied by a musical band, lanterns and other decorative items. A bystander closely watching the procession enquired about the bridegroom. He was silenced by others and was asked to enjoy the gaiety of the processions. They thought that his was a pointless question. He being a realist persisted in his enquiry saying that it was no doubt a glorious wedding party yet it was without the main character, the groom. One enquiry it was found out that the groom riding the horse had fallen on the way in a pothole while only his horse was part of the procession and no one had noticed this. In the din and celebrations no one cared for him.

What I apprehend is that the glittering spectacle of culture in both the East and West which I have witnessed in India and abroad is like the above wedding procession, without the groom. Man should be at the centre of all pursuits. However, there is no one to bother about the plight of humanity. There are few gentlemen among so many men. Very few think of other human beings. On the contrary, everyone is driven by self-interest. We all seek to help our own near and dear ones. At most, we do something for our nation which is no more than a family. Nationalism aims at caring about the people of only one particular nation. In my opinion, nationalism is useful in a very limited way.

I belong to the group that participated heart and soul in the Freedom movement. This group embarked upon this arduous mission when no one could even dream of Independence. Yet I look upon nationalism as a facet of narrow-mindedness. Concern for the whole humanity is a much more important and nobler ideal.

Let us think about Our Survival

All nations belong to the family of mankind. Concern for humanity should be our overriding concern. Which groups do work for this cause? Who is keen on the survival of mankind?

Culture, civilisation, politics, governance, literature, philosophy and all branches of learning should cater to man. If the essential humanity survives, we may take any direction or form. However, in the absence of this core, nothing will survive. Today we are engaged in killing fellow human beings. We are setting our own home ablaze. Everyone is bent upon hurting other.

Today our countrymen lack mutual love and sympathy. They are not at all moved by others' suffering. We have grown too selfish, as everyone thinks of only himself. The Qur'an states that on the Last Day everyone will flee from his brother, mother, spouse and children. (78: 34-35). The very scene may be seen even today.

Indifference to Man's Greatness

The moral degeneration rife in our country raises its ugly head whenever there is any train or air crash. Far from rescuing the accident victims, people steal their wrist watches and wallets. This alarm signal should alert everyone.

Communal riots are not the Hindu-Muslim issues alone; these betray disrespect for humanity. What ails us it that we do not respect human beings.

At times, we give more importance to trees and animals, rather than to people. We often prefer wealth to fellow human beings. Wealth is something grossly ephemeral. Yet we accord it more importance than someone's heart and soul. We do so in the face of the fact that God has made man supreme among all of His creatures. It is borne out by His identifying with man's hunger, thirst and illness. In a *hadith al-Qudsi*[4] it is affirmed thus! "Feeding a hungry person, providing water to the thirsty and calling on the sick amounts to doing good to God." Man is more worthy than all the continents in the world. Continents are there for man. Man has not been created for serving them.

Every one of us is very dear in the eyes of his parents. For they brought him up while undergoing all sorts of hardship. Our family has great expectations from us. Man is God's trustee and at the heart of this world. Yet the same man is brutally killed. His killers disregard the status of man, his parents' love for him and the energy and time invested by his teachers, and patrons. Had they realised all this, they would not have dared kill him. We have a long list of tyrants ranging from Alexander to Dara, Chengiz Khan, Halaku, Hitler and Caesar who put to death a large number of people. They failed to grasp man's worth. They were ignorant of the fact that those who cause corruption and mischief on earth incur God's wrath.

The Need of the Hour

The most pressing need today is to develop respect for humanity while

---

[4] Also called *Hadith Rabbāni,* this form of hadith is termed sacred hadith. The meaning of the text is revealed to the Holy Prophet (peace be upon him) by Allah which is expressed in his own words. See Muhammad Mustafa Azami, *Studies in Hadith Methodology and Literature* (Indianapolis, 1977).

God not Despaired of the Human Race

we adhere to our respective faiths. Let us try to reinvigorate humanity. We should greet one another as human beings. Then in the light of our study, reflection and with God's help we may opt for a way of life of our preference. But let us first promote an air of mutual love and trust. Once we welcome others, we will be in a position to move forward. If we lack this, we will not be able to communicate with anyone.

What is man? What traits does he possess? What rights does he owe to others? What is man's essential nature? Who has created man? Why has he been created? Each and every member of society should ponder over these questions. We should strive for a trustworthy ambience in the country, marked by mutual love and confidence. Incidents like those which happened in Benaras[5] should not recur.

As a religious person I hold the view that natural calamities strike us owing to our sins and injustice. God thus demonstrates that He can kill at a greater scale. We witnessed this in the storm and flood which ravaged Andhra Pradesh. Whenever there is an instance of injustice, I apprehend divine reprisal. I do not exempt anyone from this. God will assert His might whenever injustice is perpetrated. Nature takes its toll for such violations[6].

A Lone Voice Bringing about Revolution

If you have respect for mankind, it should translate into action. The influential persons, be they Prime Minister or teachers, should forego their cosy positions and come forward to save mankind. If our country does not survive, how will universities, government and democracy flourish? Who will sustain or protect them? If the country disintegrates and humanity is destroyed, only animals will be found in the UN. We must first be good human beings, imbued with the love of nation and a political understanding.

---

[5] Communal violence, according to Nadwi, destroys the prospects of peaceful co-existence. Its aftermath is a tell-tale sign of anti-humantity tendencies. Nadwi's graphic account of communal violence is detailed in his multivolume autobiography, *Kārwān i - Zindagi.*

[6] Excerpted from Nadwi, *Tuhfah i - Insāniyat* (Lucknow, 1992), 33-45. The *Tuhfah* (Gift) series by Nadwi focuses on universal values embodied in the Qur'an and the *sunnah*. These values are contextualied in an Indian setting against the backdrop of communal violence and religious anarchy.

It was imperative that those occupying top positions should have relinquished their posts in order to salvage mankind. They should have rescued their country and humanity. However, when we noted that no one was making any move in this direction, we thought of embarking on this mission. It is evident from the history of nations and also from the history of social and religious reform that at times a lone voice made all the difference as it struck a chord in everyone's heart. This eventually brought about a revolution. We have visited you in order to awaken you. Once you are sensitised, you can achieve much. Even a lone voice can help you rise to the occasion.

Chapter 3

All Creatures are God's Family

The Qur'an declares: "Allah commands that justice and excellent conduct be practiced and the kin should be given their due. He forbids indecency, evil and rebellion. He admonishes so that you may reflect." (16:90).

My elders, friends and dears ones!
The Qur'anic verse cited by me forms part of the Friday prayer sermon. Every week Muslims listen to and recite it. Since we are unfamiliar with Arabic, we do not reflect on what is recited as part of prayer and sermon. We take it only as a ritual which is part of worship. We never care to understand it or ask someone to explain its meaning. The above Qur'anic verse is indeed the manifesto, code of conduct and guideline of Islam. Allah commands justice and excellent conduct to everyone. As to giving in charity, it specifies the kin. Yet it does not insist on any particular category of kin. All those who are close to one in kinship, neighbourhood, fellow nationals or colleagues may fall into this category. The Qur'an, however, clarifies that the near and dear ones are intended.

Moreover, Allah forbids indecency and vain acts. He admonishes so that people may take a lesson.

This town of Ujjain is associated with Vikramajit[1] who is known for justice. It is reported that he was a just ruler. Today we have neglected justice and doing good to others. Justice has become rare in our times. Though it has not disappeared altogether from the world, it is hedged in by many narrow considerations.

Today justice is dispensed, based on motives and concerns. We are very particular about justice to own kith and kin, co- religionists, clan and tribe. We demand justice in their case. However, if the victim is not one of us and we may not get anything in return, say praise, we fail to deliver justice. We deny it, apprehending someone's displeasure.

For dispensing justice, we first think of a label, our own family, people, country or nation. We do not stand for justice in its absolute sense and as a religious duty. Only the pious, noble souls who have respect for humanity are

---

[1] Vikramditya was a legendary emperor of ancient India. He was characterised as an ideal king, known for his generosity, courage and patronage of scholars. Nadwi attempts to locate the emperor's personality within the framework of the *Payām* mission.

ever-ready to do justice. For they look upon the whole mankind as God's family.

It is recorded in a hadith: "All creatures are God's family."[2] This statement is explicit notwithstanding the fact that Islam makes no compromise regarding its basic doctrine of monotheism (*tawhīd*). Although Islam is so sensitive about monotheism, it speaks of all creatures as God's family. This is a radical statement. For, *surah al-Ikhlās* is reckoned as the one- third of the whole Qur'an. It deals solely with the doctrine of the unity of God. This *surah* reads as follows: "(O Prophet), say: "He is Allah, the One. Allah is unique. He does not give birth. Nor did anyone give Him birth. No one is equal unto Him." (112: 1-4)

Islam designates the above *surah* as the heart of the Qur'an and equal to one-third of the divine scripture. The same religion declares all human beings, without any distinction of their caste, colour, creed, race or nationality as part of God's family. He sustains every human being.

As to who is God's favourite, he is not the one who worships Him most. Rather, he who helps His family most. Had the idea of God's family been part of any other religion, it was understandable. However, Islam despite its uncompromising stand on monotheism, subscribes to this idea. This idea features in Islam which is God's final religion.

Justice is always fair and transparent

Allah has not directed that justice and good be done to any particular community. It should be as transparent as rain water. Only the one dispensing justice may be a Muslim or Hindu and he will be known as a just person. Justice must, however, be done to everyone, irrespective of his caste, colour or creed.

Allah commands the dispensation of justice and good in absolute terms, not to Muslims alone. Likewise, Allah introduces Himself as the Lord of the worlds, not of Muslims or Christians, Arabs or non-Arabs[3].

He has prescribed justice and fairness for everyone, including the universe, stars, the sun and the moon, galaxies, solar system of our world, continents, plants and animals. He does not believe in injustice for any nation, country or family. The Islamic command for doing justice and good is general and universal.

---

[2] Bayhaqi: hadith no. 7045.

[3] "All praise be to Allah, the Lord of the entire universe." (1: 1).

All Creatures are God's Family

Another Qur'anic directive[4] exhorts Muslims to do justice in all circumstance and their enmity towards any particular community should not prompt them to commit any injustice. They may have some grievance against a certain group or clan. However, it should not drive them to act unjustly towards them. When they dispense, they should be perfectly fair and even, grant them their due and dispense justice. For this is what pleases Allah and reflects obedience to His directives.

Let us bear this in mind that justice should be for everyone. Our Creator, Master and Sustainer has asked us to do justice and good to everyone, regardless of their community or faith. There should be no discrimination in matters of justice. Nor should anyone receive preference.

I ask Muslims that if they truly believe in Allah, they should not commit any injustice. This is our article of faith that Allah treats everyone alike. His love, sustenance, protection, and bounties are for everyone. His command is for justice for everyone. His affection for mankind is 70 times more than that of a mother for her child. He provides air, water and all other bounties to everyone, without any discrimination. He forbids any prejudice. This directive has been followed by all noble souls in all time. I have read in works on history that Vikramajit who once ruled over your town, Ujjain, was a just person[5]. Vikrami calendar is named after him. God liked his good deed and hence this calendar commemorating him is still in vogue. We know that many calendars have gone into disuse. However, the solar and lunar calendars associated with two Messengers of Allah are still followed. This does not come as a surprise to us. For their followers flourish in billions up to this day. However, the survival of Vikrami calendar underscores that God liked his good deed. As we know from history, he was a just ruler who dispensed perfect justice. We wish the same justice would have prevailed today.

Reason for the global decline and delay

The present decline and decay is on account of injustice and unfairness. Justice means total objectivity. It is like a balance which accurately weighs

---

[4] "Believers! Be upright bearers of witness for Allah, and do not let the enmity of any people move you to deviate from justice. Act justly, that is nearer to God-fearing. And fear Allah. Surely Allah is well aware of what you do." (5: 8).

[5] Nadwi highlights the enduring legacy of non-Muslim rulers who dispensed justice in ancient India. His extensive reading of history is evident from his prolific writings.

anything, including precious jewels.

Rulers, politicians, intellectuals, scholars, poets, philosophers, writers and thinkers should be perfectly just in their dealings. Had justice been prevalent in the US, the Arabs would not have been betrayed by the creation of Israel. Had justice been there in the UK, India would not have been enslaved by the British for one hundred years. Indians' estates, and crafts would not have been destroyed. Nor would have so many Indians been brutally killed by the British. Had there been no imperialism and had justice been the order of the day in our country, communal riots, grievances, court cases, strikes and demonstrations would not have erupted. Everyone then would have reaped the dividends of justice.

Two instructive incidents

Here is an instructive example of justice: In the era of 'Amr ibn Al-'Ās, the victor-governor of Egypt, there was a horse race in which his son too, participated. As a Copt outpaced him, the governor's son slapped him. That ordinary citizen went straight to Madinah, the capital and complained to the Caliph 'Umar. The Caliph summoned the governor and his son. In a public gathering 'Umar asked that Copt to slap the governor's son in the same way in his presence, which he did. It was followed by the Caliph's following remark, of which all of us should be proud. He said: "Since when have you started enslaving people, though they were born free?"[6] We should take pride in this incident and in 'Umar. We are equally proud of Vikramajit. Anyone who does good should be owned by everyone.

The other incident is of our own country which happened less than 100 years ago. There were two claimants to a land plot in Kandhla or Muzaffarnagar. Muslims claimed it to be a mosque while Hindus insisted that it was their religious site. The judge, an Englishman, listened to both the parties who had hired leading lawyers. The judge was a decent and courageous person. He asked the Hindus and Muslims to name an arbiter. They named Mawlānā Mahmud Baksh. (He belonged to the family of Mawlānā Ilyās, the founder of Tabligh Jamā'at, a globally acclaimed movement now). The Hindus held him as the most honest person in the town. This astonished the judge that the Hindus had identified a Muslim for this role. They were ready to abide by his ruling. When he was summoned, he declined, saying that he had

---

[6] Caliph 'Umar's impartial justice extended to non-Muslims. To him a governor and ordinary citizens were equal before the law. See Shibli Nu'māni, *Omar the Great*, vol.2. (Lahore, 1971).

All Creatures are God's Family

never seen the face of any Englishman. Nor did he intend to do so in future. The judge nonetheless persisted and assured him that he could testify, even without interacting with him. Such English judges were uncommon. When Mawlānā Mahmud Bakhsh arrived, he turned his back to the judge and asked him to proceed. When the judge asked him about the ownership of the site, he asserted that it belonged to Hindus and the Muslims' claim was false[7].

It is a notable example of excellent conduct. Had we emulated such role models, we would not have been lost in the present morass. The superpowers of the day, the US and Russia are highly unjust and dishonest. They care only about their own interest, not about justice. Take the case of Israel as illustrative. Its creation is a blatant travesty of injustice. The Palestinians had been living there for centuries and were the legitimate owners of the land. However, they were forcibly evicted while Jews from the US, Africa, Australia, UK, Germany and Russia were settled there. These Jews now rule over this territory[8]. This is only one of the numerous instances of injustice and falsehood across the world.

Allah commands doing justice and good. What it means is to feed the hungry, provide water to the thirsty, and call on the sick, regardless of their caste, colour or creed. As a judge, we must always act fairly. As a ruler we should treat all alike. As an official we should help everyone. Likewise, we should take care of all and share their suffering. This will serve also the cause of one's faith and prove one as a decent citizen.

Today we lack the concern for justice. Had justice been emphasised at such forums as state, radio, TV, educational institutions, social gatherings, mosques, temples, madrasahs, weddings and other celebrations, our country's fate would have changed. It would have turned into Paradise on earth. Today we go only by appearance. We do not care about truth and values.

All human beings are flowers and buds of God's garden. Yet many buds wither, with the killing of babies and cruelty to women. Who is responsible for all this? It is the devil inside us which unleashes such brutality. We are now soaked in sins. Dr Ishtiaq Qureishi who addressed you before me, rightly insisted that we all should first cleanse our heart.

---

[7] Nadwi, *Islam and the World* (Leicester, 2005), 162-3.

[8] The prolific writings of Nadwi on the Palestinian question reflect his deep study, personal experience and *ummatic* concern. His critique of the Arab world's impotence to alleviate the plight of the Palestinians is critically examined in *Western Civilisation, Islam and Muslims,* 119-22.

Paving the way in India

Our message is that we should turn into good human beings. We should reconstruct our society and pave the way for a good beginning. If a seed itself is rotten, nothing will grow. Let us first reform our country. We should sow quality seeds and cleanse our heart for good harvest. We should be mentally prepared better for absorbing good ideas. Moral teachings are not part of curriculum in our educational institution, be these primary schools or colleges or universities. Let us focus energy on moral training because man is liable to debasing himself as a beast. We neglect human values and do not love fellow human beings. We want to revert to the era of barbarism and cave life. We should try our best to transform this diseased mindset. Our Muslim brethren owe this great responsibility because of their grand claim. It is not unjustified because they have been brought into being for performing this role. It is their life-long mission to work for God's cause by way of helping victims, the weak and all human beings.

The residents of Ujjain also share this responsibility of upholding justice and fairness. They should create an ambience conducive to full freedom and justice for getting one's due and for advancing as much as he wishes. The same model should be replicated all over the country. There is no point in having animal like existence.

Our message consists in preaching justice. This is a mode of worship and essence and spirit of faith. We do not have any political ambition. It is a completely spiritual, moral, humane, divine mission resting on God-consciousness. We ask Muslims to turn into true believers and to pray. For, we are inspired in our mission by our prayer and study of the Qur'an. We urge them to study the Qur'an carefully and to offer life-enriching prayer. They should develop mutual love and unity and promote justice for all. As decent citizens and servants of humanity we should benefit others. Let everyone draw upon us. We should be like angels of mercy wherever we are. People should not let us part company with them.

All Creatures are God's Family

Gaining trust

There were some persons who intended to migrate in the wake of the 1947 holocaust[9] yet non-Muslims did not reconcile to their migration and insisted on their staying in India.

Mawlānā Liqā-Allah Uthmani of Panipat was a very pious, devout person. In 1947 all Muslims left Panipat while he stayed back. After a few years, however, he felt troubled, apprehending that no one will be able to bury him Islamically. He thought of joining fellow Muslims in Pakistan. However, the Hindu and Sikh migrants who had by then now settled in Panipat, told him that they will not let him leave the town. They would not allow any vehicle to take him. They expressed their resolve to get some Muslims settled there who would ensure his Islamic burial. Finally he stayed and passed away there.

This is a remarkable example of a pleasant life, love and excellent morals and manners. Nothing is more rewarding than love in life.

This marks the end of my speech. Other speakers will enlighten you further. If my health could permit, I could have stayed and benefitted from your company. However, I slept little last night in that we had a big program in Bhopal. My physician, Dr Ishtiaq Qureishi has warned that I would fall ill, if I do not sleep well and travel all the time. This would put you to hardship. I therefore seek your leave and request you not to rise. My brother, Shaykh Parikh will tell you further about the humane, religious, spiritual and moral way of life.

Had we lived a good life, people would have thronged to us for having a glimpse of devout persons who lead a meaningful life.

I am gratified to see this large gathering on the road listening to our talk. It is a welcome, healthy sign that people sincerely and warmly listen to our message. If people grow cynical because of political leaders' false promises, it does not auger well for our country. That you listened to us patiently and diligently, knowing well that we do not have any political agenda, is something really good and promising. I take your leave while thanking you. I look forward to a happy, positive change in Ujjain, when and if I visit it next[10].

---

[9] According to Nadwi, the wave of mutual distrust between Muslims and Hindus escalated into a genocide and millions lost their lives in the aftermath of the Partition of India. See Abdul Kader Choughley, *Sayyid Abul Hasan Ali Nadwi: Life and Works* (New Delhi, 2012), 92.

[10] Excerpted from Nadwi, *Tuhfah i - Insāniyat* (Lucknow, 1992), 60-73.

Chapter 4

When Educated People Turn Hysterical

Let me first express my happiness which is an essential human emotion. One should display his happiness. It would be something artificial to suppress one's happiness. Expressing happiness is a sign of life. For a dead person cannot vent his happiness or sorrow. As long as man is alive, he is affected by the things around him. Once he dies, his links with the external world are completely severed. He is no more moved by any happening. I cannot conceal my happiness to note such a big crowd. I am not at all embarrassed about my happiness over this large gathering.

Life: an amalgam of happy and painful incidents

Man is liable to heart-rending happenings in life. Such incidents are very much part of life. Some incidents totally break us into pieces, like a shattered glass. By the same token, certain incidents help us join our ties. Life is an amalgam of both these types of incidents. The interplay of such things weaves the web of our life.

The Most Disheartening Thing for man

Nothing is more disheartening, more demoralising and more painful thing for man than not getting someone to talk to. It is a horrifying punishment for man to confine him to a forest or a hill top where no one shares his feelings and emotion. Only his Creator then watches his condition while no one comforts and consoles him. Such aloofness is agony for man. On the contrary, if one is robbed of everything, yet if he enjoys people's sympathy and confidence, he feels happy and contented.

Hope lies at the core of our literature, fine arts, human talents, philosophy and even technology which is all about instruments. A poet looks forward to his appreciation by people. An artist sincerely does his work, without any regard for praise or criticism. If he realises that there is no one to grasp his work and his talents, he will feel much disappointed.

Treasures of Literature permeated with optimism

Our treasures of literature and library owe their existence to their appreciation. Our President is a leading writer. I have come to know reading and writing are his favourite hobby. I will take him as a witness and will ask him in your presence his response to his readers. I am not talking here about admirers. If he does not have any readers, he will hardly write. Readership is a motivating force for a writer.

Worst punishment for man

Loneliness is man's worst punishment. This thought suffocates him. God has not created man in a lonely setting. He has provided man with company. It is not part of the divine scheme that man should live all alone. Such inanimate objects as mountains, rocks and precious stones stand on their own. It is innate in human nature to enjoy other people's company. If one is confined to his own home, he takes it as a prison.

What is the nature of a prison?

What is the definition of a prison? What does it lack? Now we rule over our country. Today prisons have many facilities. There are special classes there with those amenities which are not available even in a middle-class house. Yet everyone resents to be in a prison. Why is everyone afraid of it? A prisoner is not free to meet whom he wants. He does not have even a listener. This almost strangulates him. For he cannot talk to anyone.

I have been a teacher and take great pride in this. It is a severe punishment when he is asked to sit alone at a spot and is not allowed to move around. Even if you slap him, he will overcome its pain in no time. However, it is painful for him to be confined to a spot for two hours. Even the very thought of loneliness frightens man. He instinctively wants to move around and talk. If he is denied these natural acts, it hurts him like fish out of water.

I am very pleased to see so many educated persons here, including Hindus, Muslims, Sikhs and Christians. It has enlivened me.

Man's essentially good nature

The working of the world is based upon mutual trust. It is so good to note that many people have turned up at this meeting, full of optimism. This means that man's essential nature is still good. It has been afflicted only from without. Our conscience is still in a sound condition, though we are given to using foul language. Let me add that our mind has been corrupted. This mental corruption accounts in the main for the present decline and decay. Our studies have been along the wrong lines and hence we have

When Educated People Turn Histerycal

deduced unsound results. We have misconstrued this world. Our conscience has gone into the sleep mode. However, it can be awakened[1].

I have recently visited four states. I marvel that God has gifted us such a vast, green and fertile country. We are proud of our country which is not inferior to any other country. We are fortunate to have high yield of harvest, scenic beauty, natural charms, the highest mountain in the world, long rivers and plenty of grain, fruits and above all a large population, granted to us by Allah. There is such population explosion in the country that we literally rub shoulders with others at all crowded places. It is hard for one to do shopping. Likewise, traffic control poses a serious threat.

Lack of the sense of responsibility and mutual trust and love

There is no dearth of talent in our country. However, we badly lack a sense of responsibility and civic sense. We fail to behave as decent and responsible citizens. Likewise, we do not love and trust. We suffer from the lack of confidence and fear. All this has been created by the previous government. This is a painful scenario. We ourselves are responsible for our plight. God has not been unjust to us in providing us with plenty of rain, fertile soil and grain. As a student of history and as a pragmatic person I tell you that our country matches any other country in the world in terms of intelligence, efficiency, performance, talent, common sense and basic goodness. However, not much is made of the above. So, we are deficient in all these respects.

If one does not possess anything, he has this reassuring thought that God did not bestow it upon him. Likewise, a poor, illiterate and lazy person reconciles to his fate, recognising that he is not a rich, educated and bright person. However, if God has bestowed all the above qualities on someone and still, he does not draw upon these, he feels the pain all the more. He rues the lack of opportunities. I share with you the same feeling. Among you, I am a widely traveled person in this country. Ours is a country rich in agricultural produce, minerals, and metals. Bihar is exceptionally rich in this sphere. Most of the coal is from your own state, Bihar, with a remarkable output of coal and iron. You have huge industries and refineries. Petrol, whether procured locally or by export, after it is refined

---

[1] Nadwi, *Islam: An Introduction,* 154.

here, it is distributed across the country. In sum, there is no dearth of resources.

What ails man?

Communal riots are fairly common in our country. Brothers turn into foes. People are carried away in frenzy. As soon as a mischievous person raises a provocative slogan, it seems that the whole country falls under its spell, as if they are injected by something, and they grow hysterical. Students, scholars and teachers shed their true identity. I have been to Jamshedpur, Rourkela and Ranchi after the riots had erupted there[2]. The scenes there have not only astonished but also shocked me. How can man behave so low, turning into a beast. An animal may find it very hard to transform into a human being. However, it takes little for man to debase himself as an animal. It should have been easy the other way round. For, had animals turned into humans, it must have been good for everyone. In that case we could gain something. However, it is our great misfortune if humans turn into beasts.

Stages of Man's Progress

As a baby is born, parents bring him up and offer him food which all humans take. Then he is enrolled for education and learns many role models, including his study of history containing brilliant examples. All parents, even if they may not be highly educated, try their best for the moral upbringing of their child. This is something innate in the human nature. This accounts for the phenomenal progress of humanity. Every parent wants that his child should excel him, notwithstanding man's natural feeling that he does not want to see anyone outstripping him. However, as a law of nature, every subsequent generation is more advanced than the earlier one. As a baby is fed and cared for, he is always in the human ambience. No plant, including the rose, is so much cared for, as a baby is. As he gets older, he is exposed to books and libraries meant for humans. He has institutions to cater for him. He gets an opportunity to read the best writings of the intellectuals, philosophers and scholars of the whole world. Throughout he is treated as a human being. At a later stage, he is enrolled in a school. Teachers look after him

---

[2] Communal riots and their tragic consequences are critically examined in Nadwi's autobiography, *Kārwān*. For him these riots are orchestrated by political parties and fanatical religious outfits with base desires.

When Educated People Turn Histerycal

as a human, shower affection upon him and instruct him in all that is good. We have in our midst the Education Minister. We know that the syllabus is updated every year and new experiments are carried out regularly. New theories are tested, including those originating from the US, Europe and other countries. All this is done in order to achieve academic excellence for the progress of mankind. Once that boy finishes his college he graduates and then earns his Masters degree. If he is interested, he can join a doctoral study programme. He may go abroad. These are the usual stages followed by a student.

Today we are swayed by a provocative slogan

After having received such good training what does overcome that student? There arises a wave of hatred from Patna, Monghyr, Kishanganj or Siwan, a town bordering Uttar Pradesh or elsewhere which drives even educated persons crazy. Rather, it compels them to behave as beasts. For me this syndrome is an enigma[3]. Why do people act so madly that notwithstanding their wide knowledge of philosophy, logic, moral, political science, literature, fine arts and human psychology they behave so recklessly? They turn into blood- thirsty wolves. While losing all self-control and civility they kill one another. Students and teachers spy on their colleagues, even those with whom they worked for years in laboratory and library. Why is there such a sea change? What does divest them of humanity?

Even animals have a sense of responsibility

I was in Philadelphia, near New York[4] when lightning struck the New York powerhouse. I readily realised that since both lighting and powerhouse are devoid of reason, this incident happened. But how does the communal lightning strike rational human beings? (*Loud cheers*). No one gets angry with or reproaches the inanimate lighting. Even a dog knows the cause and effect syndrome. If one hurls a stone at him, he does not entangle with that stone. He pursues his attacker, taking him as guilty. You cannot go

---

[3] "Universities should train their students in truth, honesty and guidance. Students should devote their time, energy and talent to rescuing mankind from decline and devastation." Nadwi, *The Place of Knowledge and the Role of Scholars* (Springs, 2018), 8.
[4] Nadwi's public lectures in US are largely drawn from his *da'wah* paradigm. See Nadwi, *Muslims in the West: The Message and Mission* (Leicester, 1983).

unscathed, if you tread on a dog's tail. However, if a dog is trapped in a shrub, he would not attack it.

He gets displeased with a rational being. God has granted him this understanding that every rational being is responsible for his actions. In our country a donkey is considered as the most foolish animal. Why do not we see reason?

How can man attack a fellow human being?

Please explain to me how man can attack a fellow human being? It is understandable that one may be crushed by a rock or roof or drown in a river. This may be condoned. But to attack another human being cannot be pardoned. For God has blessed him with reason, understanding, heart and conscience. He was brought up as a good human yet he has no feeling towards fellow humans.

It shocks me to observe a well - qualified office clerk, who is assigned the duty of helping those who need any paper. He is supposed to act on their request. However, as someone enters his office, he regards him as his prey for exploiting him financially. He thinks of him only as a mouse in a trap. For him the concern is to rob him of his money. This servant of God is so callous that he neglects his duty altogether. He should have warmly received that person and served him in the best possible way. For God has let him to help that person. He is a divine blessing. All his educational qualifications and hard work were meant only for helping those in need. He was sitting idle in his office and hence that person's visit should have been taken by him as a God-send opportunity.

That needy person is someone's favourite. When he fell ill, his mother spent the whole night, looking after him. She implored physicians to save her only son and offered her own life for protecting his. He was the apple of his parents' eye. However, that office clerk looks upon him as a mere prey, a mouse to be trapped and he is bent on sucking his blood. This is the ultimate nadir of humanity.[5]

-----

[5] The 'nadir of humanity' is a recurring theme in his writings about the reform of humanity.

When Educated People Turn Histerycal

An Enigma

When a wolf visits another, the former does not devour the latter. So is the case with a dog, unless he is mad. Given this, how can man attack a fellow human being? This enigma has not been explained satisfactorily so far by anyone. I want to ask you when people have this fit of violence and frenzy, one or two persons may be excused for behaving thus. However, those committing this heinous crime abandon their moral training imparted to them by their parents and teachers in schools and colleges and studies at library. How can he forget all this so easily? He appears as an educated, cultured, well - read liberal and thinker yet he is not a human being.

Education failing in imparting the lesson of humanity

Education imparts many skills to man. However, it fails in transforming him into a good human being. This is true also of the education system in the US and Europe. They do not instruct people in having respect for fellow human beings, in awakening his conscience, in instilling God-consciousness into him and in inspiring him to serve human beings[6]. Given this, even illiteracy is better than education. For the uneducated man used to help and protect fellow human beings. He would lay down his own life for saving someone's life and honour. He would guard others, keep awake so that others may enjoy sound sleep and not hurt anyone. That was a better era, though education was not so common. Today there are educational institutions in every nook and corner of the country. However, as soon as a deranged, mischievous fanatic sows the seed of discord, be it under the pretext of nationalism or communalism, he succeeds in engineering riots. I fail to think of a way how to civilise this country which is torn apart by regular rioting. Riots and decency cannot exist together. Today man is after the blood of other human beings, taking them as his prey. Cursed be such persons. Even animals and beasts are better than such pathetic persons.

Man is reformed from within, not externally

The truth is that one is reformed owing to his inner urge, not under the compulsion of any external force. We have disregarded our inner self. We

---

[6] Nadwi, *The Place of Knowledge and the Role of the Scholars,* 11-2.

do not activate our conscience. There is an essentially good human being deep inside us, with tremendous potentials and virtues. He possesses a vibrant conscience. Once this inner being appears, he can rule over vast empires. He takes state treasury as God's trust. He thinks of the entire community as its owner and himself only as a servant.

Some Bright Role Models for Humanity

I recount here two incidents. I have been a teacher of history and hence I would relate two historical incidents. The first one is about the Caliph Abu Bakr, the first rightly guided Caliph in the early history of Islam. As he took over office, he was recognised by all people as their ruler, in place of the Prophet (peace be upon him) who had passed away. At that point of time the Muslim army had been marching towards the Roman Empire in order to extirpate injustice there and to liberate human beings who were enslaved by fellow human beings. At the same time, another Muslim army was on its way to the Persian Empire. You can imagine what a vast treasury was under Caliph Abu Bakr's control. One day his wife told him: "I do not deny the tremendous benefits which Muslims have reaped after you assumed office. However, my family has suffered a great loss." On further enquiry she told: "You have fixed a stipend out of treasury for your family. It suffices only for meeting both the ends. Our family is somehow able to have only meals. We have not, however, had any dessert since you became Caliph. We want it but cannot do anything. We were far better off when you were a cloth merchant. You now hold, no doubt, an august office. But we are worse off." The Caliph replied: "I am helpless. The state treasury is for Muslims. It is not for providing dessert to us. There is no additional fund for you." She asked if he would not mind if she cut corners and save some money. He agreed on this. For days she kept spending less on daily grocery and then handed over the savings to him, requesting him to buy some flour and sugar for preparing dessert. Do you know what the Caliph did? He deposited that saving in state treasury and directed the treasury officer to reduce his stipend in that his family could survive even on a less stipend. For his wife had somehow managed to have some saving out of that stipend. So, with the less stipend his family will not still starve to death.

This irked his wife, for the stipend had been reduced, what to say of having dessert. The Caliph, however, ruled out the suggestion that his family may have any dessert[7].

---

[7] Nadwi, *Basis of a New Social Order* (Lucknow, n.d.), 9.

When Educated People Turn Histerycal

Here is another incident, which is again part of history. These are not special to any particular community. We all may take pride in these. For they were after all human beings. When the first Congress ministry was formed, Mahatma Gandhi advised: "Our ministers should emulate the lifestyle of the Caliphs Abu Bakr and 'Umar."

By the days of the Caliph 'Umar ibn 'Abd al-'Aziz the Muslim empire had extended up to Syria, Egypt, Iraq and even Spain. The whole of North Africa had fallen to Muslims. This incident is of the same period. One night the Caliph was engaged in official work, using the official lamp. There was no electricity then. He was studying and signing papers. In the meantime his friend turned up. The Caliph received him warmly and enquired about the place from which he had arrived. He asked in particular about the quality of life and supply of food there. His guest informed him that everyone had been doing well. There was no want or injustice anywhere. Then he enquired about the Caliph's family and their welfare. The moment he asked this personal question, the Caliph put off the official lamp and lit his personal one. On enquiry by the guest, he told that as far as he was engaged in public duty, it was all right for him to use the official lamp. However, once he started talking about personal and family life, he switched over to his own lamp. He could not spend public money on personal matters[8].

Can anyone cite today any such example of honesty and integrity? There are many heads of state, of the US, Russia and the Arab world. I declare it confidently that no one matches the above standard of excellence, including the heads of such Muslim majority countries as Saudi Arabia, Egypt and Iraq. No one there is so careful. For they did not receive the training which the Prophet (peace be upon him) had imparted to the Companions (*Sahābah*). I know well the people in those Muslim lands and respect them. I have comfortable stay there. I would nonetheless say it candidly that they are not up to the desirable level of honesty and integrity.

Our Loss

I urge you to feel concerned about our own country. We should infuse into everyone the spirit of humanity. Let us imbue our dear children with values.

---

[8] Accountability and transparency were salient features of the Caliphal rule. See Nadwi, *Saviours of Islamic Spirit,* vol.1 (London, 2015), 35-52.

We have already lost much. Let us do soul-searching and not blame any external agency. I am reminded here of a story which I had heard in my childhood. Someone was looking for something on the road. The passersby asked that old man as to what he was looking for. He said that he had lost his one rupee coin. They joined him in his search. They could not find it. They asked him the specific spot where he had lost it. He replied: "Actually I had dropped it somewhere inside my house. However, it is dark there while it is bright here, so I have been looking for it on this well-lit road." The same parable applies to all of us. We have lost something inside us whereas we look for it elsewhere.

You can find a lost item where you drop it

We have lost our conscience. However, we have been exploring colleges, libraries, the US and Europe, political parties, Parliament and Assemblies. The unalterable divine law is that you will recover a lost item only where you had dropped it. This law is eternal. If you have dropped something at a dark spot, take light there and you may find it. However, if you look for it at a bright spot, you will never recover it. (*Loud cheers*). I told you the above parable about a naïve old man. This, however, holds true for today's distinguished scholars and philosophers. We have lost something, deep inside our heart. However, they seek to recover it in the political and scholarly domains.

Humanity is dormant, not dead

Our conscience is dormant, not dead[9]. A lost item may be found while something dead does not come back to life. I regard humanity as dormant, not as dead. Mankind has gone into slumber many a times and been renewed as well. Messengers of Allah, scholars, sages and pious souls have revitalised mankind. Had it been dead, it could not be revived.

Even today humanity has been lying dormant. Let us revive humanity. We should begin first with our own reawakening and then call others. If we ourselves are not wide awake, we will not be able to awaken others. Those already asleep cannot awaken others. By contrast, a single awake person can

---

[9] Nadwi reiterates his call to recognise the worth and dignity of mankind. For him the restoration of humane values can effectively create an ambience of mutual trust and respect among the diverse faith groups in the country. See Nadwi, *Reconstruction of Indian Society* (Lucknow, 1974), 16.

wake up hundreds of asleep ones. If we all go into slumber, we will remain in this state for long. However, if only one takes up this cause, he can bring about a big change.

Normal conditions

We have this mission for the whole humanity. We cannot be a mute spectator to the decline of our country. This is our country where we have to live, travel and study. Our country is peopled by writers, historians and scholars. All this is owing to the normalcy in our country. Take this programme as illustrative. Had there been rain, lighting or thunderstorm or even if a snake or any other insect had appeared, you all would have dispersed hither and thither. The perfect scene now is because of normal conditions. In such an ambience we can take our country to great heights. We can carry out scholarly and scientific pursuits. We can be equal to the US in science and technology. Even we can surpass other countries. All this is a blessing of normalcy. They have achieved their progress because of this. We too, have been striving to establish normal, peaceful ambience in the country. We are not alone in this pursuit. We have explored political parties and libraries as well.

Not to Despair

Since so many people can assemble in this small town of Siwan, we are not despaired of the whole country. We think that it is wide awake and will disseminate this message to others as well. There is nonetheless a need for some hard work. Our leaders did country building. However, they did not devote themselves to nation building. Gandhi did some work in this direction. However, he could not focus on it. His successors who planned to take up this cause were lost in the morass of politics. I do not question their intention. However, this cause was neglected. This should be our goal. Let us make a call across the country for the cause of humanity and for respect for everyone. It will definitely cause ripples everywhere. People will try to exploit. You should not fall into this trap. I must tell you that the ongoing cycle of riots should come to an end forever. Immorality should be extirpated. We should take fellow human beings as God's gift and treat them as our brethren. Without this there will be no joy in life. If we learn this lesson, we will master everything.

Chapter 5

The New Generation: A Boon or Bane?

The phenomenon of birth among human beings has been on for hundreds of thousands of years. Everyday some babies are born. Today in Muradabad where we have assembled, some babies must have been born. The display of happiness in various localities of the town underscores the joys of life. This indicates that human beings have dreams and they want to lead life happily.

The birth of every baby announces that the Creator of this world, God has not still lost hope in man. He still reposes trust in him. He has not despaired of man. Otherwise, He would have stopped the phenomenon of birth. It is quite easy for Him. Take this gathering as an instance in point. It represents a modest attempt on our part. We are letting everyone in because we have organised this program for fellow human beings. That this meeting hall is full indicates that both the convenor and invitees of the program are happy. The former has been warmly receiving the latter. He is going even out of the way to welcome them.

God not despaired of the human race

Every baby born, be in India, Europe, US, the Middle East or the Fast East, declares in a charming way that the Creator of this world has not so far despaired of the human race. He wants human beings to settle down. Rather, He extends them every possible help[1]. Under His patronage we thrive. Without His support we could not survive. As you all know, a baby is born after nine months' long wait. This too, shows that God has not still given up. Were He to get angry, in no time would He destroy this world. Many wars have been waged and so many persons have tried to create havoc in the world yet they could not succeed.

In the two World Wars the mischievous elements tried their level best to destabilise the whole world. Yet it survived and possesses all of its glitter.

---

[1] This statement is reinforced by Nadwi: "Every newborn in this world declares that God has still not lost hope in man, but we go on announcing by our deeds that human beings do not deserve to walk on the earth." Nadwi, *Reconstruction of Indian Society,* 17.

Writing on the Wall

Had God not patronised this world, and had He been unhappy with humanity, the evil forces in the US and Europe, who mar our fate, would have destroyed this world altogether. Despite their organised attempts resting on science and technology, they have not been able to execute their nefarious design. It is the writing on the wall that God has not lost hope in man. He is not now about to destroy the world. Otherwise, He is able to destroy it in a fraction of a second. The Qur'an affirms: <<When He intends to do something, He says! "Be" and it becomes>>. (36:86). Only His intention suffices. Once He intends something, it is done in no time. Just as we instantly talk to someone on phone, it does not take any time for God to accomplish anything.

Do you not grasp God's intention? He wants this world to survive. But what is our response? God loves mankind whereas we are not happy with this world. God is letting babies to be born and each one of them is assigned sustenance. It is our inefficiency that we fail to provide him food on time and to his satisfaction. God has ordained sustenance for everyone. However, we betray hatred for others.

Let me talk about the recent communal riots in Rourkela, Jamshedpur, Aligarh and other towns. I want to ask as to how many harmful insects and animals have been killed by the residents of these towns. Had there been as office maintaining such record, I would have enquired the number of the scorpions, snakes, wolves, and tigers killed by the people there. Most of them, I am sure, never killed any. Yet man feels no qualms in killing fellow human beings. It points to a basic difference in God's and man's stance. God wants this world to flourish and prosper, marked by joys and His mercy and love. He is pleased with the love and understanding among people. I am happy to see this assembly. Words fail me in expressing my joy. Since God is the Lord and Sustainer, and Creator of mankind, He is gratified to note the happiness of His creatures.

Optic Illusion

The residents of Muradabad take great pride in the pots produced by them. By the same token God too, is proud of His creation. A resident of Muradabad on a visit to another town proudly tells them about the excellent quality of pots produced in his town. We too, acknowledge your expertise and accept your claim. However, are we really justified in taking credit for producing pots or machines or tailoring? Contrast this with the vast universe created by God, its diversity, and His creation of human beings. The

The New Generation: A Boom or Bane?

presence of man has invested this world with colour and meaning. Should God not be proud of His accomplishments?

All worldly subjects, be these gold, silver, pottery, computer and machinery are no more than an optic illusion. It is man who has made gold so valuable. If the use of gold is discontinued by a decision of an international convention or we decide not to have anything to do with gold, it will be reduced to something as worthless as dust. The value of gold constitutes optic illusion. It is man who has enhanced the value of this metal. We may opt for fragile glass as the most precious object in the world. There is no essential difference between a flower and a thorn. We take these as two different entities. If we decide to prefer the latter, it will be so. It is all part of the relative value fixed by us. Our inclination towards something enhances its value.

Why do prices rise? All of you are businessmen. Please explain to me this phenomenon. For the same item sells at a higher price the next day. What does account for the price rise? The only reason for this is the greater demand for a particular item. The more you buy, the higher its price goes. If you decide on not buying a particular brand of cloth, its price will crash. What is the truth behind the new fashion in clothes? Fashion originates from London and Paris and it catches people's fancy, it becomes highly popular and global. After a while, however, people discard that fashion. If one reverts to it, he is taken as someone crazy and out of date[2].

What is behind this phenomenon of being up to date or out of date? It is we who decide what is in and what is out. If we think an item to be in line with times, we regard it as up to date. Likewise, when we reject something as dated, it turns out to be out of date.

So it is man who matters most. It nonetheless appears from your conduct that you are not happy with God's will. Your will is at variance with His. God is keen on your happiness, prosperity and comfort yet you oppose this. Our attitude betrays our hostility towards Him. It is a great pity. All of us, whether be Hindu or Muslim, are religious people, with a firm belief in religious truths. However, our conduct indicates as if we are opposed to God We act against Him. For example, He exhorts us to profess and practise love yet we disregard this directive.

---

[2] Consumerism is deplored by Nadwi as it brings no joy in leading a purposeful life. See Nadwi, *Islam and the World*, 119-23.

God's forbearance

For example, if you go to a shop and disrupt its setting, the shopkeeper, who is otherwise your friend, will get furious over the disorder caused by you. He will angrily ask you as to why you did so and interfered in his arrangement. Contrast this with God's patience and forbearance. He has been regularly bringing humans into existence, and providing them with sustenance. Soil lets grain grow, the sky pours rains and the working of the world has been on, without any disruption. God does not deny us anything notwithstanding our misconduct. We should re-examine our conduct. We keep on displeasing Him. We should be grateful to Him that He does not immediately seize us for our misdeeds. Had He not been so forebearing, He could destroy this world. He has been putting up with our sins. He is not despaired of us and is not angry with mankind. On the contrary, we sever ties with other human beings at the slightest provocation. We should emulate His example in dealing with others.

God does not punish us by way of overturning our world. The cosmic laws related to the earth, the sun, the moon, clouds and rain have been constant for millions of years. We must reflect over the consequences of our misconduct.

Benefits of Learning and Knowledge

Today trumpets are blown about advancements in knowledge. The important point is whether our knowledge has benefitted us in the real sense[3]. The only advantage of our advanced knowledge is that what we used to do at a slow place, we execute it now fast, tactfully, technically and in an advanced manner. Earlier, carts caused causalities, though at a slow rate. With the introduction of train, airplane and atomic energy, death and destruction are caused at a fast pace. Is this something really good for mankind? Earlier, when a king would march on for attacking another country, he moved on horses, camels and elephants. This would alert people well in advance and they made some preparations. Today science has advanced so much that people do not get even a minute's notice. What did happen at Hiroshima and Nagasaki? Did the people there have any

---

[3] "It was a real calamity when knowledge became severed from its relationship with its Bestower. What an appalling spectacle this world presents today! Man has taken over knowledge but the Giver of knowledge has slipped from his mind!" Nadwi, *Islam and Knowledge* (Springs, 2018), 9.

The New Generation: A Boom or Bane?

warning? As to our pursuit of knowledge, it is akin to a drunkard swinging a sword or a sharp object. He is liable to kill anyone, be he his brother or a child. Today fratricide is fairly common.

Taking Risks

God has provided us with the present respite. Still our call has its appeal. People are drawn towards truth, simplicity and sincerity. Likewise, we do feel others' pain. There are many thinking, sincere persons. However, no one has the courage to take any initiative. Everyone does not turn hysterical in a riot. Nor do they become mad. What nonetheless happens is that some mischievous, Godless persons dominate the scene. They have no sensitivity for other human beings. As a result, decent persons retire to background. They fail to take on the wicked, apprehending their humiliation and loss. Thus, the decent ones are confined to their homes. There are good people in every town and village. However, they are too timid and hesitant. The wicked thus have a field day. They do not fear God. With the decent one retiring from the scene, fearing their humiliation, no one comes forward. However, if we respond thus, the working of the world would suffer. Risk has to be taken.

An Eloquent Example

Most of my experience is derived from religion. Our Prophet (peace be upon him) has related to us an example. I have not still found any other excelling it. For it is very graphic and eloquent. We must gather courage to stem injustice, oppression, anarchy, disorder, mischief and corruption, no matter how hard and painful it might be. If we do not prevent it, we will not survive. The Prophet (peace be upon him) gave this example: <<There is a boat, with many people on board. It has an upper and a lower class. Some are in the former and others in the latter class. Water is stored in the upper cabin. It is not easy to draw water directly from the river. It calls for equipment and effort. Those in the lower cabin go upstairs for taking water. It is natural that water splashes as it is carried. When those in the upper cabin noted this, they objected, pointing out that it put them to inconvenience. For their clothes, floor and other belongings had been spoiled by the spilled water. They stopped them from carrying any water. Those staying downstairs could not survive without water. They resolved to get it and thought of boring a hole into the boat for getting water from that river. The Prophet (peace be upon him) added: "Had they possessed

understanding and love of life, they would have helped those staying downstairs. They should have implored them not to dig a hole in the boat. However, they neglected the hole in the boat, thinking that they will be safe upstairs and let those downstairs suffer. However, once there is a hole in the boat, everyone will be drowned, whether staying upstairs or downstairs. If the boat sinks, everyone will perish."[4]>>.

Today our society, not only of India but of the entire 20th century world, resembles that boat, boarded by both upper and lower-class passengers. The former being high browed people resent everything and assert their elite status. They suffer from superiority complex. As to the latter, they resort to corruption, hoarding, black marketing, dishonesty and neglecting duty. Workers do not work yet demand higher wages. As to their employers, they make them work hard yet they try to pay them bare minimum. Everyone is after his own interest. Indirectly everyone is digging a hole and flooding the boat with water. God has gifted us with both mental and physical power. If intellectuals, scholars, patriots and nationalists neglect their duty and turn a blind eye to the mess around them, it spells disaster.

As a boat gets filled with water, it is bound to sink. Once it sinks, all will drown, without any distinction. When fire erupts in a village, it does not differentiate between the house of a Hindu or Muslim, between a pious and a wicked person and between the rich and the poor. It is a blind force that destroys everything which comes in its way. The same holds true for the flood which does not discriminate between the rich and the poor.

Our Society on the Decline

Today our society is on the decline. Many passengers on board are engaged in sinking it. They are fishing in the troubled waters. Look at the situation in government offices and railway stations and even in our housing colonies. Everyone is self-centred, having no interest in nation building. We are after only our own gains, without any concern for others' plight. Everyone subscribes to the view that he alone should benefit.

Let me recount to you an instructive story. There was a king who built a pond and asked everyone to pour a pot of milk into it and charge him the price of milk. Each one of the people thought that if he would pour a pot of water, rather than of milk, it would not make any difference. No one will be able to find out as to who had put water instead of milk. So each one did so. The king arrived the next morning, thinking that the pond will be

---

[4] Bukhari and Tirmidhi.

full of milk. He was feeling on the way proud of this feat. However, he was aghast to see that the pond had only water. Each one had cheated him.

This is the main problem, as all of us think of unfair means. We may make some exceptions. For this is the divine law. Nonetheless, the trend for cheating is on the rise. All of us are concerned only about our gains. We should fear Allah and not act dishonestly. But we care only about short-term gains and have no sense of our accountability to God.

What ails us is that each one of us is keen on grabbing some benefit. We may get some benefit but it destroys the social fabric[5]. We are faced with moral decay. We think that it is very intelligent on our part if we make quick money. It is definitely not an intelligent act. Self-restraint alone fills our heart with true happiness. If we seek only to gratify our base desires, it will not bring any happiness to us. Our own society will turn into a curse for us. People will then wish for death in order to escape their misery.

Life-in-Death

A morally decayed society has a strong wish for death. You will find around you many with the death wish. This life-in- death is horrible. On the basis of my study of literature I know that greed, love of money, use of unfair means and following base desires lead to spiritual starvation. People tend to feel like fish out of water. Everyone has the choking feeling. It is a pity that today the law abiding and pious people have not won recognition whereas those who violate law have their way. So even the law - abiding people give up the straight way.

Nadir of our Society

I receive many visitors who seek my advice, taking me as a religious person. Many persons have told me that they are stigmatised in their workplace because they do not accept bribery. It is an irony, for we should have looked down upon those given to bribery. We should have instinctively expelled such immoral elements from our midst. But we turn inimical to honest, truthful persons. Even the evil persons feel the pangs of conscience on observing an honest person who does not indulge in bribery. However, they do not want to see any pious person in society.

This represents the nadir of our society. For we have turned averse to good

---

[5] Nadwi, *Basis of a New Social Order*, 19.

and the law - abiding persons feel isolated and alienated.

All of us are Fellow Passengers

We all are fellow passengers. Some persons are bent upon sinking the boat. The process of sinking has begun. Total destruction may take some time because our country being a large one is like a big boat. So the signs of the impending disaster may not be visible to you. You do not have a clear idea of the damage already caused and at what points. As you know, ours is a vast country, with a population of millions. So, it may take some time. The delay is due to its huge size.

Facing Extinction

Please note that ours is a huge country. We should be grateful to God for this favour, though we do not appreciate it. One of my friends, an acclaimed scholar originally from Hyderabad, is settled in Paris[6]. Both of us participated in a conference in Geneva. We were on the way to airport. I had my international passport and hence could visit any country. I had visa for Germany and France. My friend, however, abruptly stopped on the way, saying that if we moved further even within that airport, we would enter Germany and it will be then difficult for us to return. What I want to underscore is that some countries in Europe are so small that you can cross these by car. Here in India it takes even three nights train journey to reach Bangalore or Calicut. It is a great blessing. However, it entails responsibility as well. It is our duty to keep our country in order. As I warned you, some people are bent upon corrupting. Can we give them a free hand to do as they wish?

We together have to steer our boat to safety and take care of our country. Otherwise, we and our country would be lost in oblivion.

Injustice cannot prosper

No country vitiated with injustice can ever prosper. This moral truth should be brought to the attention of our ministers, scholars and leaders.

We have witnessed the fall of many rulers in our country. It appeared that

---

[6] Reference is to the internationally acclaimed Islamic scholar Professor Muhammad Hamidullah (d.2002). A polyglot, Hamidullah made immense contributions in the fields of *tafsār* and *sirah* literature.

the British will never leave India. The then England was a super power. The sun did not set over the British Empire. They had perpetrated injustice. In your own town of Moradabad they had put to death hundreds of Indians. However, the same British rulers vanished into thin air one day.

God does not put up with injustice

God does not bear with injustice, committed by any religion, political party, sect, or society. If any group or class thinks that by killing the innocent, unleashing injustice, crushing babies against wall and throwing people into furnace would help establish their supremacy, they are totally mistaken. The sooner they overcome this delusion, the better it would be for them. God let us do injustice. However, those guilty of it never prosper. Injustice cannot be a way of life, which we painfully note these days in India. A human being is pleased to note others happy. Even scorpions and snakes have cordial relations among themselves. Wolves move about in a pack. What kind of people are we that we cannot put up with fellow human beings? Are we afflicted by some fit?[7]

Innocent Victims

We see a traveler arriving in Moradabad, for visiting his mother or for providing sustenance to his wife, or returning home from Mumbai after having earned some money there with his hard work. That innocent person is stabbed to death. We do not care as to whom we killed. The victim was someone's very dear one. His mother had milked him with much hardship. God had provided for his sustenance. When he fell ill, hectic efforts were made for his cure. He was imparted education. However, when he was able to earn his bread, an enemy of God and mankind and a grossly unjust person stabbed him to death, without realising the disastrous effects of his ghastly act[8]. He never thought as to how his shocked family will react on seeing his dead body. How will the killer show his face to God? An unjust tyrant is deaf and blind to all these considerations. I do not regard such wicked persons

---

[7] Nadwi describes this fit a 'whirlwind of butchery and destruction'. Human beings are slaughtered either for a trifling object or religious fanaticism. Nadwi, *Reconstruction of Indian Society*, 16.

[8] "Therefore, we ordained for the Children of Israel that he who slays a soul unless it be (in punishment) for murder or for spreading mischief on earth shall be as if he had slain all mankind..." (5: 32).

as Hindu or Muslim. It amounts to discrediting Islam, if a Muslim kills an innocent person. I am sure that the same holds true for Hinduism. These religions have nothing to do with such callous killers. Though they may pledge fervently their loyalty to their faith, such criminals do not profess or practice any faith. God's curse is upon them. He hates them. Their heinous crimes have nothing to do with faith. For faith does not teach such misconduct of killing innocent persons.

More Bloodthirsty than a Jaguar

That innocent passenger had left railway station. He was full of dreams, and of meeting his mother, wife and children. They would have been delighted to receive him. He had brought gifts from Mumbai for each of them such as shirts, shoes, sweets and his savings. All of his dreams were shattered. That beastly killer, more horrible than thousands of jaguars and more accursed than thousands of snakes and scorpions, killed him, without caring about anything, his dreams and his family. No religion in the world can honour such a horrible person.

He deserves deterrent punishment. Even those hitting him with shoes will turn impure.

How to Prosper?

Do you think that with such misconduct we can ever prosper? Do these misdeeds draw us towards God and promote love and cordial relations? Will these help us prosper and gain a place in the comity of nations? When we go abroad, such reports bring shame to us. When I visit overseas, the people there ask me about the high incidence of riots and disorder in our country. Can I reply to them, saying that it is all owing to ignorance and with the advent of culture, knowledge and God-consciousness, things will improve? When will this change happen? We have been waiting for this for so long. There has been no improvement for ages, though we saw the emergence of many reformers. Muhammad Ali and Shawkat Ali[9], hailing from the vicinity of Moradabad, strove hard for Hindu-Muslim unity. Their mission had a spell over everyone, which I had observed firsthand, like many other

---

[9] Both brothers were political activists who strove for national unity. Mahatma Gandhi undertook a countrywide tour in the company of Muhammad Ali and Shawkat Ali, "addressing mammoth public gatherings from place to place and arousing the masses for the national struggle." See Nadwi, *Muslims in India*, 117.

The New Generation: A Boom or Bane?

countrymen. I was then only 10-11 years old. It was owing to God's mercy that the whole country was then united. Hindus and Muslims had been very close to one another. Had that spirit survived, ours, would have been a different country. It was a golden period of cordial community relations. However, the British caused discord among us. Lord Harding hatched a conspiracy and made us fight among ourselves. Since then we have not seen any Hindu-Muslim unity which was once the order of the day. Today I can see a glimpse of the same friendliness. For you have assembled in large numbers, regardless of your faith and sect. You have gathered here to listen to someone whom you do not know and who is not a very worthy person either.

Long Slumber

Yet we should not despair. Thank God, our countrymen are dormant, not dead. Let us thank and praise our Lord and Creator for this. For an asleep person can be woken up whereas a dead person cannot be revived. We have fallen asleep many times. However, we then rose to the occasion. Same holds true for mankind. Once we wake up, we will compensate for all of our loss. I am sure once we get up we will apologise to others for our offences and implore them to forgive us. For as asleep persons we were not aware of anything done unknowingly. Presently we are in the state of a deep, long slumber.

I regard those rioters as persons in a slumber. I do not dismiss them outright as devils. The inner goodness has become dormant while their bestial instincts have surfaced. Let us strive to awaken their goodness and eliminate their bestiality.

Are Reports about Riots Our Only Business?

We do not have any illusion about ourselves that we will bring about a major revolution in the world. We are aware of our limitations. However, we cannot sit idle either. Is reading reports about riots our only business? Should we silently watch the degradation of humanity? In that case we will be the most wretched people. Instead of only reading reports about disorder, let us take some action[10].

---

[10] The media has the potential through disinformation and propaganda ploys to fan the flames of communal violence. In many instances Nadwi was the object of ridicule by the media for his steadfast principle to safeguard the constitutional rights of Muslims.

I had launched this mission in 1951-52, after my overseas visit. On watching the worse situation in the country, I could not sit idle. I made a call with my articles to this effect. Then other causes engaged me. May God pardon me for these lapses. I should have given it the top priority.

Let me conclude now. I took very long. However, I have the satisfaction that I have spoken truth and shown you a mirror to see your own face and plight.

Chapter 6

Peaceful Co-Existence

A Herculean Task

You have assembled here from all parts of the country at the call of *Payām i - Insāniyat*. My colleagues and I realise that owing to the paucity of time we could not gather a bigger audience. For there are many in every nook and corner of our country who would have responded to our call. Our country has been famous for this cause. So many people could assemble here who would have outnumbered the total population of Lucknow. We would have still welcomed you. Anyway, at a short notice we invited people from various parts of the country. Those whom God enabled have assembled here. You all must have noted their fervour.

Perhaps you think that peaceful co-existence is something simple and easy. You arrived here safely, listened to the speeches and will now return home. Do not take *Payām i - Insāniyat* call as a magical pill which will solve all problems. And this is true of not only India, but of all places, including the holy towns of Makkah and Madinah that peaceful co-existence is not easy anywhere. Same applies to the holy towns of Hindus. Much effort is needed for living peacefully with others. Please do not think that our mission is only about inviting people and they may assemble here, after incurring expenses on their travel. Do not be under the delusion that after this program there will be peace and happiness everywhere and riots will come to an end forever. Man is man and life is unalterable. Man has been behaving in a certain way for thousands of years and life has its perils and challenges. Man is not an angel and accordingly he will earn God's greater reward. He will honour us. Man will get such a reward which will make even angels jealous. Man is liable to err, something which angels cannot do. Man is liable to get angry, and many times. However, he is able to control his anger and repent afterwards. With all these peculiar traits we should exist peacefully with others in every locality, town and country. You should not have this misconception that after this program there will be no friction, quarrel or dispute. We are subject to disappointment and loss in this world. Likewise, we have to put up with much which we do not like. Yet we have not despaired of man, of the human nature and of our country. We cannot move out of our country, even if we will so. There is no room for us on any planet. Nor does any country have space for us. We are to face all problems, conflicts and obstacles in our country. More importantly, we have to resolve all the issues and amicably set our disputes with others. This is our task which is very tough. We will settle down in the same town, as equal citizens and good treatment for everyone. We will lead our lives in dignity and as well-meaning gentlemen.

Morals should govern our conduct

Anyone observing the cordial atmosphere and friendly speeches at this assembly should not think that now all problems will be over. There will be no more fighting or conflicts. Anyone having such daydreams should better realise that real life is quite different. Anything may happen at any time. Since there are opposing elements, friction is bound to happen. In the presence of mischievous elements even a small friction may flare up. There are, no doubt, forces of construction and goodwill in our country. However, owing to various factors, destructive and destabilising forces are also at work and they will try to implement their agenda as well. In his speech a few minutes ago, Shaykh Abdul Karim Parikh illustrated the character and working of Satan. Satan can create trouble over trivial issues. So there are forces around us which are hell-bent on causing discord. They will continue in our midst. However, we should not lose our poise. Let us not act childishly. We must exercise self-restraint. Morals should cover our conduct. We should behave stoically. We have outlined in our speeches how we should act with self-respect. I do make allowance for human feelings. Yet we must practise self-control and try to influence others as well along the same lines.

Messengers' Contributions

The best role model in this context is of Messengers of Allah[1]. When they appeared on the scene, there was not a soul to listen to them. Nor did anyone grasp their message. They thought that they were in the company of beasts. The Qur'an records the following response of a community to whom the Messenger of God had presented his call: <<They said: "Most of what you say is beyond us. We are unable to grasp anything. We do not know what you are talking about. What we note is that you are the weakest person in our midst. Given this, why should we listen to you?">> (11:91). More important, however, is the Messengers' response. A Midas touch turns a rock

---

[1] According to Nadwi, Prophethood is intrinsic to humanity's progression for moral development. See Nadwi, *Islamic Concept of Prophethood* (Lucknow, 1976), 8-38.

into gold. So is the case with alchemy which transforms dust into gold. Messengers enable human beings to excel even angels. They infused such piety and self-control into their followers that in the absence of hard historical evidence one could not otherwise believe in their feat. Even their die-hard enemies who were after their blood turned into ardent admirers of those Messengers. They were ready to lay down their lives for their Messengers. Those who came with a resolve to assassinate these Messengers embraced their message after interacting with them. For they spread the message of love and peace among those who were given to violence and bloodshed. These Messengers welcomed even killers into their fold and cleansed them. This led to a big change in society. The period of moral decay was replaced by that of spirituality and religious fervour. The life-giving message of faith became the order of the day. We have been still drawing upon the Messengers' accomplishments. I firmly believe that all good, love and light which prevail in the world today is owing to their message. We may attain much progress and even go up the sky yet we would realise that the standard of patience, humanism, mercy and love set by Messengers is the highest. Their role model presents before us higher benchmarks.

Love of money behind rioting

We will soon part company after the speeches are over. However, please carry this message wherever you go that we all have to replace destruction, hatred, hostility and immorality with construction, love, peace and morality respectively.

Our country is afflicted with this menace: love of money. This has been eating into the vitals of our country. For our selfish gains we can go to any extent. I append the same love of money behind the rampant rioting in our country. I may be mistaken in my assessment but I suspect that jealousy and narrow-mindedness are also at work.

Let us face reality

We must take into account these ground realities. Let us not while away our time in a fool's paradise. Let us note the ground realities: corruption has vitiated our entire system. With this menace we do not need any threat from without. For corruption suffices to enervate us. Our country is akin to an insect-infested huge tree which may collapse any moment notwithstanding its apparent big size. As a citizen of this country and having spent all my life here, I am in a position to make these observations.

Our society has been sapped of its vitality. In my speech in Lucknow, I had said: "All truths have lost their meaning in our country. The only forces at work are: love of money and communal hatred."

The Danger Confronting Our Country

I publicly say this with all the force at my command that our country is in peril. Bribery, immorality, and slavish mentality are rife everywhere. Things were not so bad even during the British rule. The British had enslaved only our body. Today, our mind and our conscience are enslaved. The worst form of slavery is human bondage when one lords over other human beings. Worse, each one of us is intent upon making most of any opportunity by using unfair means. We treat fellow citizens worse than what the British masters did to us. This is evident in court, police station and other public places. I may be forgiven for this candidness that the same affliction mars even our educational institutions. Slavish mentality is the order of the day.

Our Country Divided into Two Camps

Today the entire country is divided into two camps. People brand these as the camps of Hindus and Muslims. For me, however, there are two camps: of the ruler and the ruled, and of the seller and the buyer. We have turned indifferent to the misconduct of rulers. Our hearts have turned hard. However, things have now come to such a pass that even an ordinary citizen lords over and humiliates other citizens. They behave worse than the British. Whoever is in power exploits others. We realise all the time that we are not independent, no matter whether we are traveling by train, air, at the railway platform, in park or while studying in a college or university. We do not enjoy any respect. When we return from abroad, we face humiliation on arrival. This is something utterly shameful that I might feel comfortable and independent while in the UK, US or Saudi Arabia. However, on returning home we are made to realise that we are still slaves. We have to put up with all this. The miserable scenes are aplenty at airports, railway platforms and police stations. Every Indian feels that he is not still free. He feels alienated while talking to his own brother, child or fellow citizen. We have turned into strangers for one another. This situation is not natural which should be reversed immediately.

Peaceful Co-Existence

Rampant Disorder

Our *Payām i - Insāniyat* mission is not only against the recurrence of communal riots. These riots occasionally erupt. We are more concerned about the disorder in every home, the corruption in our society and the all-round malaise around us. Let us stop and prevent it.

Not an Easy Path

The above path is long and difficult. It is full of thorny obstacles. We have to surmount all hardship. I do not want you to suffer from the delusion that on return from this assembly you will find your society totally transformed, with only love and peace in the air. It is quite likely that on the way back home you may undergo a very bitter experience. For such unpleasant incidents are fairly common. Worse, we ourselves are responsible for this. The Qur'an states: "Corruption has spread on land and sea. This is because of people's own deeds. They will taste the consequences of their actions. Maybe they return (to truth)." (30: 41)

Corruption has pervaded land and sea, and mountains and caves. According to the Creator of man and his nature, this is on account of his own deeds. We are given to the love of wealth. As a result, we do not recognise the ties of kinship, not fear God, not respect human beings and not value man's worth. We take everyone as a customer or a prey.

Loss of Humanity

I note that as a citizen approaches a government office, the staff looks upon him as a prey to be robbed of his money. Far from receiving him properly and serving him, they disregard his plight and misery. They are only after his money and demand bribery. A shrewd customer promises bribe, thinking that by bribing him he can get anything done. Is this the face of humanity? Is there any joy in such life?

The Nadir of Humanity

Those present here have a hard task ahead of them. On your return you will confront bitter realities and will have to exercise much self-restraint. I have made my point in my speech. Man is liable to committing lapses and he often falls a prey to his base self. Yet our newspapers, writers, columnists, political parties and leaders still keep on provoking people. They incite people's anger. Leave them alone and do not incite people. Their own anger itself is a serious problem. It should not blow any further. Let us act carefully. Our journalists, political leaders, teachers and government officials should realise that they are dealing with their own countrymen and their own children. They are not aliens. We should not be hostile towards them. It is shameful that we disgrace one another. We have created money yet we worship the same. It is an abysmal scene to witness the obsessive culture of cheating, bribery and dishonesty. Let us remember that man's heart is the recipient of divine refulgence and the human mind has illuminated the whole world down the ages.

Maintain Links with Values

Being a student of history, I have read about the rise and fall of many empires and the downfall of several forces. No one has been powerful forever. No one can exercise absolute power in future either. Every rise has its fall. We have been a witness to the decline of many. Those in power today will bite the dust tomorrow.

Let us do soul-searching and recognise our status. Do not forget that death is constantly after us. God continues to enjoy absolute power. He has His heavenly forces. At His single gesture, we will be obliterated. Our own bombs may bring about our annihilation. We may take pride in our vast country. However, this will perish in no time. Let us turn to God, the Ever Living One. We should gain His understanding.

Our Message Reverberates the Prophet's Message

Let me make this important clarification. The *Payām i - Insāniyat* mission is often associated with me. It is popularly known as my mission or movement. Let me state it clearly that it is not my mission. I am simply nobody. I myself need this mission. If I transgress the limits by way of losing temper, please ask me to behave properly. This mission is actually the Messengers' mission. It was presented by noble, truthful souls and is meant for the whole mankind[2]. It is a call for humanity towards a humane way of life. I am a poor mortal who would not be around after some time. So do not ascribe it to me. It represents the Messengers' mission and hence it may lead to divine blessings and mercy. Please attribute this mission to the

---

[2] Ibid., 88.

Peaceful Co-Existence

divine scriptures so that our efforts are accepted by God. This movement should be associated with pious and sincere persons.

Spread this Mission across the country

I am gratified and thankful to you. On behalf of my colleagues and friends I thank you that at a short notice you undertook long arduous journeys, neglecting your important business. This, however, makes me feel optimistic. Humanity is still alive. I am not a political leader. Nor do I hold any important position. I am only an ordinary worker, with some interest in scholarly activities. My colleagues, who are professionals, made this call and you were gracious enough to respond to it and assembled here. Now onwards this mission should be very dear to your heart. Please transmit it across the country. It is not only our mission. Please infuse self-restraint into fellow citizens. It is an alarming trend that people believe in rumours and even improbable things. It is a new allergy which affects our nervous system. People get provoked in no time. Let us give up this behaviour pattern. God has made us trustees of this vast country. Much merit and talents are called for undertaking this onerous responsibility. It requires also strong faith, hard work, maturity of thought and discernment. Let us develop these traits.

With this message I seek your leave and thank you and also on behalf of my colleagues all those who organised this program at a short notice. They deserve credit for having arranged such a big gathering. The presence of so many listeners indicates that humanity is not dead and we need not despair.

At the end we praise Allah, the Lord of the worlds.

Chapter 7

Joys of Life Filled With Love

Man needs love most in life

I am grateful to the President of this meeting and other respectable persons present here. For they had not seen or heard me earlier yet they reposed trust in me and spoke highly of me. I feel gratified by their compliments. These are a source of inspiration for me. Man does not need only food, clothes and money. He needs love most. If one does not get love, and possesses all else, he feels as if he is in a museum, watching everything yet having nothing. One receiving love and affection forgets even his suffering, fatigue, anger and sorrow. Man is always after love, mutual trust and he appreciates it most. I am therefore thankful to you all for having trusted me.

The Malaise Afflicting Us

The most serious malaise afflicting our society is that we do not trust one another. May God forgive our politicians, enable them to do good and direct them to the right path. Our political leaders have lost their credibility. They have made us distrust everyone. One fears to open his mouth. Today it is incredible that one may say something selflessly. The worldly- wise people always assume that there must be some motive behind what we say. Some are more tactful and express themselves only at the opportune moment. Some say it too hastily. The shrewd ones state their intention only later. What is important is that people have lost credibility and mutual trust. Though it is my first visit to your town, I am indebted for having reposed confidence in me. You trusted your brethren who told you that I will share some good points with you. And you gave up your business and assembled here in large numbers. This has boosted my morale. This is what makes the world going. Otherwise, we are confronted with a disgusting situation which may drive us mad or force us to go into exile. It is such a depressing scene everywhere. We have despaired of mankind. Life rests on the ray of hope. It is so gratifying that you trusted me. I had no link with you. I had not met you earlier. Most of you do not read newspapers and magazines. Nor would you be familiar with my books which may have reached only some madrasahs. Yet you chose to listen to me. This underscores your faith in humanity[1].

A Parable

Let me, relate to you a story about a saint, known in Delhi as Sultanji. The locality in Delhi, Nizamuddin is named after him. He is more famously known as Nizām al-din Awliyā. Someone brought a pair of scissors in his session. Upon spotting it, he said: "I do not need it. I am not here to cut or tear anything. On the contrary, I link hearts. I do not tear hearts asunder. Better give this a pair of scissors to someone and bring me a needle for sewing. I am here to draw people together, not to repulse them."[2]

Divisive Forces

Many divisive forces are at work presently. Fragmentation is highly common. Even our tongue has turned into a sharp weapon. I am devoted mostly to academic work and do meet a cross section of people. For me, politics is the biggest divisive force. It is too extensive, too sharp and too far-reaching. A politician has his impact across the country. Divisive forces work overtime in the national and state capitals namely, Delhi and Lucknow. Every political party is engaged in divisive activities. This nefarious work is carried out by every political leader, journalist and writer. Man is supposed to use his tongue for promoting and reinforcing love and kindness. This was, however, the case in yesteryears. Today everyone is in the morass of sectarianism and divisive politics. We use our tongue for sowing discord among people, for shedding blood. Same holds true for our pen. Pen is another tool for bringing people closer. This was, however, the practice in the past. We are now given totally to abusing and defaming others. Both tongue and pen are now abused for fanning hatred and violence.

---

[1] Nadwi wrote several books devoted to the issues of reform of the Indian society. The *Islāhiyāt* genre is representative of this theme and has resonance for societies afflicted by the scourge of corruption and violence.

[2] Nizām al-din Awliyā embodied in his personality moral excellence and the spirit of humanity. For an elaboration of his life and mission, see Nadwi, *Saviours of Islamic Spirit,* vol.2 (Lucknow, 1974), 147-256.

Joys of Life Filled With Love

The Power of Pen

The Editors' Conference held in Lucknow some time ago was addressed by our Prime Minister[3]. She had inaugurated it. Some of my friends brought her to Nadwah. Both Hindu and Muslim editors were present at this august conference. I was asked to speak. I related to them a classical Persian couplet which reads thus: "Tread softly, for many will be hurt by you."[4] Pen controls the fate of millions. That poet had only few persons in his mind. But, with the recent advancement in journalism and its ever-growing impact, it has assumed great importance. A journalist should be better addressed as His Majesty. The range of media is wide and vast. Journalists now exercise the same power which was once enjoyed by kings. However, if they turn to a destructive course, its impact would be far-reaching. I therefore urged editors to take great care in using their pen. For much discord today is owing to poisonous writings[5].

There are many noble souls in our country who have promoted love and understanding. I have been to many countries, including some distant ones. I have visited many Muslim countries. However, these champions of mutual love and cordiality are not in such large numbers in other countries. Being a student of history, I am very fond of reading books on history. Rather, it is my hobby or passion. We learn from history that some of these saints came to India from distant places. Some of them were natives. They strove hard for establishing peace and fraternity. I recounted to you the incident related to Nizām al-din Awliyā. He loved humanity. On reading the account of saints, we learn the meaning of love. These saints had respect for fellow human beings.

The Poison Killing Our Society

It is a general tendency that one's weaknesses are attributed to his religion. The followers of a religion are given a label, even if a lapse is committed by only an individual. That person is not a representative of his community or religion. What accounts for this attitude is the poison which has seeped into

---

[3] Reference is to Indira Gandhi.

[4] In a similar vein, Nadwi would express his candour in his meetings with Arab royalty. His advice to them focused largely on moral regeneration in their respective countries.

[5] Nadwi, *The Country on a Dangerous Turn and the Responsibility of Intellectuals* (Lucknow, n.d.), 14.

our mind, which has, in turn, vitiated our system, our milieu, and our entire society. There is an urgent need to detoxify. If it is not done, our life will become difficult. Far from being a saint, I am only an ordinary person. However, God has invested man with the discerning ability to forecast future happenings. It is like one's assertion about the impending rain on noting lightning and storm. His above assertion is certainly not some prophecy. Rather, it is an everyday occurrence. By the same token, the daily happenings around us indicate that in the absence of any deterrent action, our society and country would be destroyed soon[6]. For the hostility, misperceptions and hatred permeating our society, literature, educational system, philosophy and politics do not augur well for our country.

The Philosophy of Fear and Hate

A leading European philosopher is on record having remarked: "If you want to keep a community under your control, do not let them become extinct. Rather, use the psychosis of fear and hate against them. Make them afraid of someone and keep them quarrelling with others. By employing this strategy you will maintain leadership and enjoy power uninterruptedly."

C.E.M. Joad is the author of these two works: i) *Introduction to Modern Philosophy* and ii) *Guide to Modern Wickedness*[7]. He was the Head, Department of Philosophy at the University of London. He is famous for these two thought-provoking books. He adds that if you are unable to find a community for infusing fear and hate into others, invent one, including a celestial or imaginary one. Invent an enemy, be it a star or the sun or the moon, fish or river, as an object of hate before your followers and make them fearful of it. This will help you enjoy power and control. People will be lost in fighting or fear while those in power will not face any challenge. If our country is destroyed, how can we survive? We may win an election, grab an office or win some popularity, yet we will face the horrible consequences of this poison. We may confront this danger in our own life time. Or it may strike in the next generation of our own children.

Man loves his children most. He works hard and invests money for them.

---

[6] A similar warning was given by Nadwi in his speech (1960) to the Muslim elite in Burma (Myanmar). They were mired in vulgar extravagance and an opulent lifestyle that betrayed streaks of materialism. A military revolution and Communist takeover dealt a severe blow to the minority Muslims. See Nadwi, *Kārwān*, vol.1, 456-9.

[7] Nadwi quotes these books to highlight the inherent weaknesses of Western civilisation in his celebrated work, *Islam and the World*.

Joys of Life Filled With Love

If we plant an orchard, we know that we may not get its fruits in our own lifetime. We know that we are investing it for our children. This long term planning is innate in the human nature. Think of your children. It this hate and fear continue, though our generation will pass away in 60-70 years, the plight of our country would be pitiable. We have to be careful about the atmosphere which our children will inherit.

Seeds of Hatred Sown Everywhere

It is common knowledge that a farmer sows seeds, which results in the growth of plants and then he reaps harvest. Same holds true for the crop of hate and fear. This crop grows wildly and fast. Once the seeds of hatred and fear are sown, one will have a huge yield, higher than that of any grain such as wheat, maize, barely or paddy. Today the seeds of hatred are sown everywhere in our country. One community is fearful of another. They try to hide their fear as well. This is a symptom of a complex. One who projects himself as a lion-hearted person betrays sheer cowardice. Let me do some plain talking. Hindus and Muslims fear one another. They hate and fear one another at the same time. Yet they cover up their fear. For they do not want to be exposed as coward. If you dig deep into their psyche, you will note this mutual fear. Every citizen is in the state of fear. Be assured, you need not fear me. Hindus and Muslims fear one another because of the lack of mutual understanding between them. They have never explored love which God has bestowed upon them.

Our Weakness

If we let everyone to love, it will grow and deep bonds of love, as between mother and her child, will develop. However, since there is a lack of communication between Hindus and Muslims, they cannot develop any mutual love[8].

Our history, literature and poetry are suffused with love. Yet the same love is not allowed to flourish. All channels of communication have been sealed. The only outlet is of hatred. While love is not allowed to prosper, hatred has a field day. For winning election and for gaining power, a

---

[8] Nadwi reminds Muslims to take the initiative to restore the bonds of mutual trust and love. Co-existence, however, does not imply compromise of the corporate Islamic identity. In fact, the reconstruction of the Indian society should take priority over other considerations. Nadwi, *The Country on a Dangerous Turn,* 12.

politician resorts to the divisive politics of hatred. He makes people fight against one another. In contrast, the one promoting love and peace is asked to retire from the public scene. He is bluntly told that he is not needed and that he should stay at home.

In my opinion, this is our main weakness. If one appears at the stage and delivers a fiery speech inciting Muslims thus: "O Muslim brethren! See the injustice done to you in this country. The Hindus are bent on crushing you. They would not allow you to live with dignity." His outburst will render my presentation null and void. My friends will only keep watching him while he will cast a spell on the audience. He will turn popular instantly. Likewise, if another speaker turns up who incites the feelings of Hindus and alerts them against Pakistan and its designs, the audience will abandon the speakers and chair of this forum. The crowd will then not listen to anyone. This is our weakness which is responsible for our present plight.

This weakness is owing to our laxity in that we have given a free hand to those who exploit human beings. These mischievous elements know that the easiest way to fool people is to fill into them the seeds of hatred and fear. This gives them control over people. As to those who preach love and self restraint, they have no listeners. Only few persons respond, and that too half-heartedly. This is the danger looming over our country.

If this trend continues, there will be no one to attend a meeting like this. In the next twenty years you will not get any response at all. God has given you a chance now. So work hard and learn the lesson of peaceful co-existence. All of us together should try to rescue our country. Let us appreciate the bounties which God has lavished upon this country. Regard it as your own country and love everything of it. Learn to live like human beings. Then you will enjoy life. You will appreciate even if you do not have money. You will be happy with even limited resources.

Miracles of Love

A family blessed with love enjoys life, even though they may be poor. They enjoy sound sleep and have a good time. In contrast, the families riven by quarrels, litigation, and jealousy have no peace of mind. They are apprehensive about murder, robbery, public humiliation and court cases. A family may have a huge bank balance and all amenities like TV and other luxury items yet they have no joy of life. They do not have any time for leisure and for family life. In contrast, there are homes without any amenities i.e. TV, radio, excellent crockery, finishing and decoration. Yet they are blessed with mutual love and happiness. A large family with four sons and two daughters lives happily, full of sacrifice and affection for another. They receive warmly their guests and visitors. Social relations keep them occupied. Elderly ladies lavish affection on the young ones. The seniors motivate and guide their juniors. They follow centuries-old custom of patting on the head and touching the feet. On observing their life one realises what the joys of life are, even with meagre resources. For the rich with their plentitude do not have so satisfying lives.

Lead Life Marked by Love

Let all of us learn to lead life, which is marked by love. Then we will find out what it means. The constant fear of one another has made our lives miserable. People in one locality are terrified of those in another. Colleagues, though working on the same desk do not trust one another. They apprehend that the other one may lodge a complaint or get him implicated in bribery. This is if the messy condition of our offices, localities and institutions. Those entrusted with moral education and character building are themselves mired in corruption. Our educational institutions may be of good quality. However, we know that the colleges and universities in other towns are not up to the mark. They have lost their credibility. Students do not respect their teachers and the latter have no affection for the former. Rather, they stand as two opposite enemy camps, bent upon destroying each other.

I need not elaborate more. We all should assimilate basic human values. We were imparted this lesson first by God's Messengers. They had been sent down for the same objective. These Messengers had their companions and disciples. Then there were saints and devout persons. I recounted to you the instructive incident related to a noble soul. Someone presented him a pair of scissors of good quality. He, however, declined, saying that the mission of his life is to unite people, not to hurt them. He was devoted to the cause of bringing people closer to one another. This is a simple message, devoid of any complex philosophy. Today our country needs love, trust and understanding. Divisive forces[9] are already at work in every village, town, locality, school and madrasahs. What is needed now is the message of

---

[9] Divisive forces assume the form of political parties with rabid ideological positions, extremist religious groups or individuals with vested interests. They promote factionalism among the masses to advance their nefarious designs.

mutual love, help and support. Our country has many models who promoted love and trust. We should respect and appreciate others. Still we have some noble souls who selflessly work for the welfare of humanity.

An Incident

Once we were returning from Atraula. Our friend, a physician, was driving. We had been there to attend a friend's wedding. As we left, a vehicle carrying a young veiled woman, hit our car. She fell down and fainted. Our friend being a physician was carrying medicine. A little later she gained consciousness. In the meantime, all the villagers assembled on the spot. That we had no animosity against that woman had no meaning for them. We were on our way to Lucknow. However, there stood a crowd before us, carrying sticks. We had nothing to do with them. We did not even know which village it was. The situation could soon take a communal turn and we could be killed. However, a teacher appeared on the scene. He seated us and assured us that no harm would be done to us. He did not let anyone move towards us. He took us to the nearby police station and was keen on bearing all the expenses. We told them that we had sufficient money. Someone bluntly asked him as to why he was protecting us while we were Muslims and he was a Hindu. The questioned him about his kindness to us. He replied: "We all are human beings. May God protect them." We never met him again. However, our country is proud of such noble souls. This ensures happiness and peace in our midst. We want to carry the same message in every nook and corner of our country. This message should be imbibed by all Hindus and Muslims. This is the very purpose for which we have arrived in your town.

A Lone Voice

It is a matter of concern for us as to who would listen to our lone voice. There are so many newspapers and public meetings. We are able to address only two to three hundred persons in this town. Will it suffice for bringing about a revolution? However, this is how a beginning is always made. If one thought only about his limited reach, no cause could be taken up. Take our Freedom struggle as illustrative. The leaders of our Independence movement, Gandhi, Ali Brothers and Motilal Nehru did not have a large following in the early stage. Millions did not initially turn up at their meetings. It was after a long time that their mission received mass support. So it is a single seed which makes the difference. Were every farmer to think alike that it is futile to sow a few seeds, there would be no grain in our country and we will starve to death.

Build Mutual Trust

I urge you to create an ambience of love and trust. Our Scripture, the Qur'an presents the outline of an ideal society. In the context of a baseless allegation against someone the Qur'an asks the believers as to why they did not repudiate that charge. For since they could not do such a wrongdoing, they should not have expected one of them to commit it. We should have an ideal society in which everyone should think highly of others. This thought should not occur to us that one of us could do any wrong. The Qur'an seeks to create such a healthy, trustworthy society[10].

We should have such confidence in others that we should not be even prepared to hear anything against them. This is a common human lapse that we readily buy a negative story about anyone. When we shop, this equation is based solely on mutual trust. Same holds true for our relationship with a physician, with the belief that he would diagnose well and cure us. As a student approaches a teacher, he holds the belief that the latter is well informed and will impart him best education. Trust binds us to fellow human beings. In its absence our society would collapse like a pack of cards. Our society will be then sapped of life.

This is our message to you and to the whole country. This is what has brought us here. This is the essence of *Payām i - Insāniyat* mission. Since all of you are educated people, I do not have to elucidate any further.

Please promote mutual love and trust make our country, India a paradise on earth.

Chapter 8

Mutual Trust and Peace

I am extremely happy and feel honoured that so many of my brethren have assembled. I have got a wonderful opportunity to interact with and talk to you. The organisers deserve credit for having assembled at such a short notice so many people of various communities and sections. This underscores their kindness and sincerity of purpose. Let us all rejoice in it and thank our Lord that in response to a single call many have responded. This meeting does not promise any feast or entertainment. Rather, it is a program with a particular mission. That it has drawn a big audience indicates that there is ample scope and potential for our mission. I feel much optimistic. People still have trust in one another.

Normal Conditions Are a Great Blessing

Let me congratulate you on this assembly. However, it is all owing to God's help. First, there is pleasant weather today, without any storm or lightning or rain. There is normalcy in your town. Had you worked very hard and used all means for organizing this program, implored everyone to attend it, visited every house and pleaded for their participation, lightning and rain or any law and order problem, God forbid, in any part of your town would have ruined all your preparation. So your commitment alone is not to be lauded. Good weather is another contributing factor. Also, normal conditions account for the success of this program. Without such normalcy, even the most famous speaker, most accomplished scholar, a Vice Chancellor of a university, our Education minister or even an overseas scholar could not attract any audience. Had the conditions not been normal, or if the weather would have been inclement and people had felt anxious over weather, law and order or safe return home, all the efforts of organisers would have been in vain. Even a handful of persons would not have then gathered here.

The point I want to press home is that though all accomplishments, feats of merit, sincerity of purpose and sparks of genius are important in their own right, nothing can be achieved if the atmosphere is not conducive. Normalcy of conditions and a pleasant milieu coupled with sound and safe law and order situation are essential. Rather, these are a great blessing.

Love and Peace

You all are sitting under a canopy. By the same token, there is a bigger, overarching canopy resting on strong, formidable pillars. That is the canopy of law and order, love and peace, and mutual respect and trust. We know by experience that man is not like a deadly snake or scorpion. We join one another's company knowing well that we will be safe. For we are not in the company of wolves. What to say of any intrusion by a wolf, I have seen in some public meetings that notwithstanding the presence of a highly competent speaker who is holding the audience under a spell, a rumour about sighting a snake disturbs the whole gathering. Without verifying facts, people disperse in panic, running hither and thither. No one considers that it might be a ploy for sabotaging the program out of political vendetta. The speaker who had captivated everyone is abandoned. All efforts to pacify the panic-struck people fail. The announcement that it is only a rumour has no effect. No one thinks that the appearance of one snake cannot inflict much damage anyway. Volunteers try their best to control the situation. However, there ensues a melee, injuring some persons.

Peace: A Precious Blessing

The success of a public meeting should not be credited only to the speakers or organisers. Those inviting people may be respectable, credible persons. However, pleasant weather too, is a contributing factor. More importantly, normalcy owing to a good law and order situation is another component of this success. Peace is a great blessing bestowed by Allah. However, we forget this. Let us not forget that all achievements in the domains of literature, poetry, science and technology and philosophy have been owing to a peaceful, conducive atmosphere.

We know that two World Wars were waged. Many books have been written on these wars. I would nonetheless request a scholar to study as to what accomplishments were made during the War period. Of course, these wars had not ravaged every nook and corner of the world. All the countries were not exposed it. There was no worldwide bombing. Yet people in general were anxious. They had lost the peace of mind. They were sceptic about the survival of the world. Some took these as the imminent Last Day. Hindus and Muslims believe in this doctrine, though they use different terms to designate it. In sum, people were then unsure of future. They thought it was pointless to marry, to compose poetry, or to strive for a feat, since nothing was certain. The very future of the world was at stake. Take the world literary masterpieces such as *Ramayana, Shahnameh* or great works of Arabic and Persian, or the poetical works of Ghalib, Mir and Sauda or of other poets of Delhi and Lucknow, all these owe their existence to normal conditions of life. Normalcy must be maintained at all costs. People should have mutual trust and respect. Everyone should be confident about the security of his life and honour. I have many friends and relatives in Gorakhpur, with old ties. I have been here several times. At their kind invitation I arrived here and was received warmly. However, if I had the slightest apprehension about any dishonor or trouble here, I would not have come here. Everyone is naturally very particular about his security, honour, home, children and country. If they are in danger, one loses all joys of life. He does not then pay any attention to poetry or any other hobby. He cannot concentrate on his religious duties. Nor is he drawn to committing any sin. One enjoys life most when there are normal conditions.

Follow the path of moderation

Our first and foremost duty in our country is to maintain peace and normalcy, mutual trust, a sense of security and an urge to strive. One should have the inspiration to accomplish something for himself, for his children, for enhancing his knowledge and for enriching this world. One should have motivation to enlighten others, and to express his love for them. God has given talents to each one of us. He has blessed us with the zest for life. We have opportunities for self- expression. If a physician tells someone that he would not live any longer, all words of comfort and consolation fail. Anything interesting, say a story, a poem, delicious food, or a festive party will not attract him at all. He will lose interest in all that is around him. He will feel as if death will overtake him any moment. He would feel too weak and lifeless. Having lost confidence, he appears as a totally different person. Same holds true for those sentenced to death. A jailor will endorse that such convicts lose interest in everything.

Our First and Foremost Duty

The first and foremost duty of citizens in a country is to ensure normalcy and good law and order situation. People should have mutual love and respect. They should get opportunities to actualise their potentials. God has gifted everyone with some sparks which should motivate us. We should enjoy the bounties of this world. Without the peace of mind, trust and security one cannot enjoy anything in life. No philosopher can revitalise a sceptic.

On visiting a hospital, one notes pale faces in acute depression. Though they are not on deathbed they appear lost and despondent owing to the ambience in hospital. If you move a patient to his house, his engagement with children and others and his moving away from the sick all around him, he feels much better. In contrast, if a healthy person enters hospital, he is taken aback by the atmosphere there. For only diseases, health issues and medicines are discussed there. He sees everyone having medicines and injections and there is nothing to cheer up people there. There is no celebration. On the contrary, people are engrossed about the well - being of their near and dear ones. Everyone is concerned only about health issues. So even a healthy person starts feeling depressed. It goes without saying that hospitals provide much relief. Hospitals in Europe have very good facilities, including nutritious food. People there prefer hospital to home. This is because of a different atmosphere in those hospitals.

What Ails Us?

The truth is that God has lavished upon our country numerous bounties. Great, noble souls have been born here. God has not deprived us of anything. Yet we have not proved ourselves worthy of the divine favours done to us. We have not appreciated divine blessings. We have fallen a prey to greed. We want to grow rich overnight. Earning money is not bad in itself. This is a natural human trait. However, the love of wealth has afflicted us as an epidemic. Each one of us wants to turn into a wealthy person is no time. This is our malaise. Our literature, press, fiction and popular magazines have whetted our appetite for quick money. We are trapped by consumerism. We want to buy all luxury items such as TV, refrigerator, cooler etc. In the past, people earned wealth at a slow pace and they had to work hard for it. There were few rich person then.

Now wealth can be amassed in no time. Illegal money by way of bribery is now fairly common. It makes people rich overnight. One gets a huge windfall without doing any hard work. A needy person bribes those in authority and since both need each other, they get what they want, without any trouble. So one gets illicit money worth thousands of rupees easily. The needy person is in a hurry and for saving his time he makes payment on the spot. The one grabbing this easy money procures luxury items. His family gets soon TV, fridge, radio, cooler etc. This was not the case earlier. Getting money used to be a lengthy process. One working hard for a long period of time managed to get some money. Now everything is quick and fast. People turn rich overnight. This is our main ailment. On getting up one fine morning one tends to flourish as a rich person.

Mutual Trust and Peace

Life: A Game of Chance

In our times lottery has become highly popular. It attracts millions. We come across reports that someone turned overnight into a millionaire. It has changed the fortune of some persons. This has affected our psyche. Not only do people take a chance by buying lottery tickets, they put at stake everything for amassing wealth. So doing, they disregard nobility, civility, self- respect and other values. The love of money has overtaken people in Asia like a curse. People have transgressed all limits in their craze for more and more money. They want to get rich at any cost, even by way of murdering humanity and values.

I have noted painfully that one approaching a government office needing help is badly exploited by staff. They pay no heed to the misery of that person. Nor do they have any sense of duty in trying to solve his problem. They are concerned only about extracting as much money as possible from him. They have their eyes set only on the amount of bribery which they would get while oppressing that needy person.

The Root Cause of Our Malaise

In my considered opinion, the love of wealth is the root cause of our plight. We want to grab money, fair or foul. Our whole society is getting corrupted. Corruption was there earlier as well. As a student of history, I know that there have been vices in all eras. People are liable to cheating. However, the corruption of the whole society is something unprecedented. For it spells disaster. As Romans fell a prey to corruption, they met with their decline and fall. Nothing could then salvage them. The Romans were acclaimed for their law, literature, philosophy and culture. However, nothing could save them. They collapsed like a diseased, hollow tree at a slight gesture. They were lost into oblivion.

Unity in Diversity

We all have to live together in this country. Those who wanted to go have emigrated while those left behind are here to stay forever. Take our clothes as an instance in point. All fabrics are interwoven and then it becomes usable. By the same token, all people are bound together in a society. You should not have this wrong impression that you can survive in isolation from others. Those belonging to various faiths, classes and talents are part of the same web. Our fate is interlinked. If the majority of people are evil, the good ones should not think that they can live with them. Their condition would be like that of fish out of water, as it cannot exist without water. A pious person, be a Hindu or Muslim, cannot be comfortable in a corrupted society. It is like a sea wave which is active only within sea. The moment it comes out of sea, it vanishes. It is instantly absorbed in sand. Life is like a fast-flowing river, of which the waves are interconnected. One should not assume that he is good enough and that his home and locality are marked by piety. There should be an overall atmosphere of goodness and virtues. An island is always located within water. Indonesia is a living example, as it is a network of islands. We cannot live like an island. That would be patently unnatural. Our fate is bound together. If we all are good, irrespective of being Hindu or Muslim, it augurs well for us.

A Muslim should not have this mistaken notion that his prayer, fasting and his shunning lies and bribery would suffice. If one is pious as an individual, it is fine. However, there is no guarantee that the children of that pious person will be able to protect themselves in a degenerate society. One deserves credit for withstanding the corruption around him. However, his subsequent generations will not be safe. So, everyone should feel concerned about the moral disorder. We should think of reforming the whole society. For one is very much involved in his society. He would be exposed to cheating and lies in offices, and educational intuitions. Even the latter are devoid of values. One fails to note any of these features there: integrity, working hard for passing examination, teachers instilling hard work and discipline into students and lavishing affection upon them, students' esteem for their teachers and pursuing studies diligently. One feels suffocated in such a decayed society. Every thinking person will have this feeling. It would be surprising of one does not resent this unhealthy ambience.

What Astonishes Me

I am astonished as to how life goes on in this choking atmosphere. People are busy in setting up new political parties. Newspapers keep reporting about all-round progress, peace and security. No one cares as to what is actually going on. You may get a true picture on interacting with train passengers. Travel, be it by train or air, is full of hardship. So is the inefficient functioning of our offices. While people want a quick response to their requests, government offices take months to act. One cannot get his lawful work done without bribery. Brazenly the staff would tell you to expect any action only when you bribe them. I have the firsthand experience of my society. I too, have to get many things done. There is mess everywhere.

The Enemy From Within

Times have changed and it is no longer possible for a foreign country to invade. That era is, thank God, over. It is not likely to come back either. Generally, there is no interference in the internal affairs of any country. However, the biggest threat is posed by the enemy from within. The external invaders have left our country a long time ago. However, internal problems plague us. We have fallen a prey to evil. Cheating pervades our society. It has become our second nature. Given this, we do not need any aggression from without. We ourselves suffice for tormenting, harassing and humiliating our own countrymen. The foreign ruler had his own style of functioning. In dealing with them we faced much disgrace. However, we were then a slave nation. But today we face humiliation and hardship at every step. No one had expected this turn of events. So no one is happy about the present state of affairs.

No rejoicing on returning home

Let me frankly share this experience with you. I do not rejoice when I return from my trip abroad. We may visit Arabia which is very dear to us owing to our religious link with it. However, as human beings we should feel happy on returning home from Arabia. If we do not feel happy, it would be very unnatural. We may go to Arabia frequently and we love that land in view of our bond of faith. But, after all, we are Indians and should rejoice on returning home. For back here we speak our own language, use our dress, meet our friends and relatives. We know our place too well. For we were born and grew up here. All this is perfectly natural that we should be glad when we return home.

However, our society has degenerated so much that even Indians are afraid of returning to their homeland. I share this only with you, not with outsiders. For it will be too embarrassing for me to discuss it with them. Let me tell you in all honesty that when my plane lands in Mumbai and I return after months after being in some Arab or European country, I do feel excited. My friends and family stand outside to receive me. I would hug them and on reaching home I will get food of my own taste. I will resume my routine life. However, on landing I apprehend that disgrace which does not stare me in the face when I land in any foreign country. In Europe it is fairly common to see the sign at the customs counter, "Nothing to Declare". They trust you. At most they would ask you and then let you go. But at Mumbai airport they rummage through your luggage, open every box and search for the dutiable items everywhere. I have seen them checking the ink inside fountain pain in order to ensure that it is not filled with gold. In Europe they recognise you a scholar, educated person and appreciate the purpose of your visit, say of delivering a lecture at a university. It satisfies them fully.

Here at Indian airports no one accepts my version of the purpose of my visit as a member of some academy or committee. The custom officials insist that all pieces of luggage should be opened. I am interrogated about the items I have brought from abroad. If you give them a fountain pen as bribe, you can cross the customs counter easily. Otherwise, you will be held up for hours. You may be hungry, worried about those waiting outside for you. Your friends may be there for hours in the car park, partly owing to the late arrival of the plane. You are detained further. You cannot go unless you bribe them. Your credentials have no meaning for these officials. You feel that you are a criminal, not a scholar or an educated person. They will not recognise you as a well- wisher of the community and humanity. What a great pity that foreigners do not have any suspicions while your own countrymen doubt your integrity. There is a common feeling of distrust here. They look at you with suspicion. Only after an enquiry they may concede that you are a gentleman.

We ourselves are responsible for this sorry state of affairs. Many Indian travelers have been guilty of smuggling gold. Custom officials are justified to an extent in assuming every traveler abroad as an offender. Given this, one does not feel happy on returning home. This pain surpasses his joy of his reunion with family. One's apprehension about humiliation depresses him.

The Last Nail in the Coffin

We have made a mess of our own country. God has not been unkind to our country. He has blessed us with everything. Yet we have ruined it owing to our misconduct and our excessive love of money. Those after making quick money get success. The recent advance is science and technology has made it easier to get rich in no time. As a result morals, religion, human values and all other considerations have been relegated to margins. Everyone is after his own gains. No one is interested in noble ideals, or the doctrine of the Hereafter. While following the Epicurean way of life everyone is after only enjoying life and amassing wealth.

Mutual Trust and Peace

Our Responsibility

Let me warn you that no one from outside will set things right for us. We cannot afford to have another foreign rule. The very thought is disgusting. Our country has benefitted the world much in the domains of mathematics and philosophy. People from overseas have been here and gained much. During the Muslim rule, our Indian scholars went to Makkah and Madinah and taught there. They disseminated vast treasures of knowledge there. The scholars of Makkah, Madinah, Egypt and Syria acclaimed the expertise of these Indian scholars. So we cannot even think of the presence of outsiders in our country. We have to do something and set things right.

The first and foremost point is that we should maintain normalcy, as all achievements are possible only when normalcy prevails. We should strive to curb the current trend for the love of money and the resultant decline and decay. All of you should launch a campaign against it. Ours is a vast country and we alone cannot accomplish everything. We may, however, resolve today that we will not commit any evil now onwards. We will not indulge in any injustice. Nor will we hurt anyone. We will extend every help to everyone and serve others. This is our message to you. This is what *Payām i - Insāniyat* stands for. Let us be humane persons. This will fill our life with abiding happiness.

Importance of Justice and Excellent Conduct in Society

Allah command justice, excellent conduct and giving in charity to the kin. He forbids manifest indecency, evil and injustice. He exhorts you so that you may take lesson.

(16: 9)

Importance of Delivering the Message at a Public Meeting

We are used to having academic sessions at a hall, marked by silence. The ambience in a Seminar is usually of pin-drop silence, with the highly attentive audience. I am, however, very happy that this meeting is being held in the heart of the town market[1]. For I believe that if a message does not become a topic of public interest and debate, it is not likely to create any ripples. Our weakness is that we discuss issues which are confined to madrasahs, mosques, temples and traditional Hindu educational institutions. We tend to be like an island on sea. You, however, go unnoticed. If you discuss something while flying, only a few seated next to you may be able to listen. You would be mistaken in thinking of having conveyed your message. For it will not attract any attention. Your discussion will remain restricted to that plane.

Truth is still acknowledged universally. People do present and listen to a good message. However, if it is directed at the select few, or in a remote corner, it will not have the desired result. Those who move about in the elite, select class have no impact on ordinary people and ground realities. The message should be addressed to the common people. As an academician I prefer a calm and quiet place for study, without any disturbance. So by my training I should have felt upset for being asked to speak in a market. I should have been disturbed by this setting. However, I have learnt some lessons from experience. Accordingly, I am happy for being given this opportunity. I would rather like this practice to continue. For, what is stated within the confines of mosque and madrasah or at times at radio station should come to public domain.

---

[1] Some of Nadwi's important books were written in the third-compartment of trains which were teeming with commuters. The disturbance normally associated with traveling did not affect the tempo of his writing. Choughley, *Sayyid Abul Hasan Ali Nadwi,* 62.

As long as the issue of the freedom of our county was discussed in closed door meetings, libraries and scholars' chambers or in the study rooms of intellectuals, thinkers and philosophers, it made no difference in the ground situation. The British government was unmoved by this discourse. However, when public meetings were regularly held and the issue of Independence was hotly discussed in parks, markets and other public places, the same British establishment was shaken to the core. This happened at a time when the British Empire had its sway over almost the whole world and the sun never set in this empire. So this is a good trend of organising these programs on roadside, in market and other public places.

Need for Peace and Normalcy

Presently the world stands, so to speak, on the verge of a volcano. Let me tell you something basic and essential. At the moment, you are listening attentively to my speech. Should it rain, you would not sit any more. Same holds true if a stray animal barges in this meeting. The important point is that only in normal circumstances people listen to the message of religion, morals, reason, and justice. If there is no normalcy, with terrible conditions on the ground, say lightning and heavy downpour, even the best speaker in the world will not receive any attention. His profound wisdom will not be of any interest to anyone. This is the normal human response. Only when one is at peace, in normal, peaceful circumstances, has no fear or pain, he listens carefully. Even if he is hungry or is disturbed from within or without, he loses his interest and attention. Only in a peaceful setting he listens and follows. Otherwise, no incentive or threat can prompt him to pay any heed.

We want normalcy to prevail not only in our country but in the whole world. This will enable everyone to devote to his pursuit, be he a teacher, writer, poet, artist, intellectual, scholar or scholar. Each one of them will then accomplish something. It is worth-noting that literary masterpieces were produced in normal times. One suffering from stomach ache would not be able to deliver a speech either. One may persuade him much, yet he will not like to hear any couplet. Nor will he enjoy it at all.

Importance of Justice and Excellent Conduct in Society

What is Amiss in Our Times

God has lavished numerous bounties upon our country. Yet we are unable to execute things on time. Nor are public demands met. If you have any business or a journey ahead, you cannot move without bribery. God has devised a perfect scheme of things. It is possible for man to enjoy life much. He can have what he wants. However, it calls for love and peace, efficiency, punctuality, no fear of robbery or theft. One without any worry enjoys sound sleep. Likewise, in normal conditions one may travel across the whole country without any concern for safety and security. He may openly carry gold from one place to another. Scientific and technological advancements have helped man control even weather, diseases and long distances. Man has explored space. Despite all these achievements we have not still attained our real objective and true purpose.

What is the reason? We have made machines but not good human beings. There are not competent men to make the best use of machines. You know well that when good men were around while machines were not there, there was peace and happiness in the world. Recall the golden age of Vikramajit. People still fondly remember him. Your town, Ujjain is very famous. For Vikrami calendar was launched in your town in the days of the king Vikramajit. At that no machine was there, as for example, this amplifying microphone, radio, TV or any other gadget. Yet people were thinking and listening men. Even without microphone, radio, or electricity they did listen to the message originating from a far-off place. More importantly, in their own interest they followed that message which was for the good of everyone. Today the problem is that with the help of gadgets you can transmit every good message across the world. However, there is no one to listen. There is no one interested. Everyone is mad only about making money, having luxury items and attaining name and fame. There is a constant tussle for power and position. No one has regard for anything else. Given this, what is the use of such luxury items? Rather, these cause more harm. Evil-minded persons abuse modern gadgets.

We believe that virtues will flourish and they are protected and guaranteed only when there is healthy, pious milieu. When life in general is on sound principles, when those visiting and having transactions in market are pious, when they are God- fearing and full of love for others, there will be all-round happiness. Then virtues will prosper. There are hundreds of universities in our country. However, these are sites of violence daily. Students do not want to learn. Teachers are not interested in imparting knowledge[2]. The former want only degrees and the latter only salary. Academicians admit that there is no academic atmosphere on the campus. Even if teachers want to teach, students are not interested. They seek only degrees, without attendance and even without examination. They want the higher qualifications of BA, MA and LLB while they do not want any examination for earning these degrees.

The Callousness of the Selfish, Money-minded Persons and the Decline of Humanity

Resources alone do not suffice. The important thing is the soul. If man's inner being is purged, he will have a robust conscience. He will then use things properly and will manage with little or even no resources. Messengers of Allah accomplished much, though they had meagre resources. Today, even with huge resources we are unable to achieve anything. Luxury items now dominate us. We are subordinate to these. The very things meant for helping and serving man have enslaved him. Worse, we follow them blindly and even at the expense of crushing fellow human beings. We trample upon dead bodies of people in order to gratify our base self[3]. There are many who on being told that they will get money or promotion only if they crush other people, they would do so without any qualms of conscience. We have been debasing humanity. This wickedness is re-enacted every day. Humanity is constantly disgraced and crushed.

Have Respect for Humanity

Our message is that all of us should cultivate respect for humanity and maintain cordial conditions for accomplishing all that is good. Otherwise, we are doomed. If the ambience is not good and we are in a morass of decadence, we will lose everything. Normalcy is essential for doing good. Otherwise, rumours will disturb and destroy everything. In an era of decline there will be no one to deliver a sermon. For there will be no listener. Once an earthquake strikes, everyone loses poise. Likewise, when fire breaks out, even parents abandon their own children. People had turned too panicky during the two World Wars. We therefore insist on peace and normalcy. We

---

[2] Nadwi makes reference to Muslim scholars in the recent past whose commitment to teaching was unparalleled. No monetary incentives could persuade them to abandon their low-salaried teaching position. Nadwi, *Islam and the World,* 164.

[3] The bane of amassing wealth and using it for illegal purposes is the key theme in Nadwi's critique of society. See Nadwi, *Kārwān,* vol.5, 200.

Importance of Justice and Excellent Conduct in Society

during the two World Wars. We therefore insist on peace and normalcy. We should have love and respect for fellow human beings.

Kalidas[4] was born in your region. He was a great poet and is acclaimed up to this day. He enjoyed peace and normalcy. He was therefore able to compose his masterpiece which is read now as well. We are keen on normalcy in our country so that moral teachers may impart morals, teachers may disseminate knowledge and people may be imbued with human values.

Blessings Accruing from Justice and Excellent Conduct

The following Qur'anic verse was recited before you: "Allah commands justice and excellent conduct and giving in charity to the kith and kin." God urges us to practise justice and excellent conduct.

Justice consists in having what is one's due. However, excellent conduct demands giving others more than what is their due. Also it stands for being just to one who had done injustice to you. This is what good moral conduct is. It is prescribed by all religions. Islam constructed a society in line with these ideals. On reading early Islamic history one comes across this instructive incident.

Someone sent a food dish as a present to his neighbour who passed it on to his neighbour and eventually it came back to the one who had sent it in the first place. Another incident is more life-ennobling! On the battleground, a badly wounded Muslim asked for water. As it was presented to him, he gestured that it be given to another injured person lying next to him. When he was offered, he pointed to another wounded person, insisting that it be given to him first. By then all of them passed away, without taking a drop of water. They have, however, left behind a living example of perfect morals. This is how noble souls behave. They preferred to lay down their own lives in order to help others[5].

---

[4] Kalidasa was a classical Sanskrit writer who lived during the 4th-5th century. His epic poems and plays are primarily based on the divine scriptures of Hinduism. Essentially, he was a moralist who advanced the cause of humanity. Nadwi reiterates the need for normalcy to nurture the production of literary works like Kalidas.

[5] These incidents of self-sacrifice by the *Sahābah* are intended to raise the moral consciousness of humanity. As opposed to self-sacrifice are self-centred traits that vitiate the dynamism of society. Se Nadwi, *Islam and the World*, 33-61.

Selfishness: Root Cause of All Problems

The real malaise today is that each one of us wants to serve his own interest, even at the cost of someone's life and plight. This is the root cause of all trouble. What is the scene in our trains? Robbery, looting and inefficiency are rife. No one is getting his due. Things are not done on time. There is a mess everywhere. Post office and telephone services are in shambles. Train services are mostly non-functional. People have become devoid of any sense of duty and responsibility. How will our country pull on?

Man is the only victim

Today we hate one another. I ask the killers of other human beings: "How many scorpions have you killed in your life?" I am sure that they did not ever kill a single scorpion, snake or wolf. Fellow men are their only victims. Do they not fear God at all? Is man more worthless than a scorpion a snake or mouse? Even mice damage man's belongings. But they do not kill them. Their hands are stained with the blood of only human beings. They never killed any beast. However, they display their bravery in killing men. They know well how disastrous it as to pluck even a single flower in a garden[6].

No owner of a garden will be reconciled to damaging his single rose. Given this, will God bear with their destruction? Were one to damage a potter's pots, he would face its horrible consequences at the hands of that potter. How can they then destroy God's wonderful creation? God's creatures are more beautiful and more worthy than Taj Mahal. Man is God's creation. They should fear God while destroying His creation. Were one to even touch Taj Mahal with an evil intention, he would be severely punished. Even the archaeological ruins, which are in tatters, cannot be damaged. Is man more worthless than these? Our country cannot survive if communal riots, bribery and inefficiency are not curbed. Even superpowers of the day cannot survive with such degeneration. Likewise, if they support a country mired in such problems, it will make no difference. One himself can set his

---

[6] Nadwi deplores the state of lawlessness in the country. For him tyranny is ruinous and invites the 'wrath of the Creator of the universe who inflicts chastisement, calamities and afflictions on the perpetrators." Nadwi, *Violence and Tyranny* (Lucknow, 1995), 3-4.

house in order. Let us mend our ways.

Why the Emperor Vikramajit Enjoys Everlasting Fame

India has been ruled by many kings. However, among them the emperor Vikramajit enjoys everlasting fame. His devotion to justice accounts for his renown. He dispensed justice during his reign, as history books reveal. He was a virtuous ruler and hence enjoys such fame. In this town which is associated with him I urge you to maintain peaceful, normal atmosphere so that everyone may do what he wants, be it the academic activity of teaching and learning and spreading some message or serving the homeland or worshipping the Lord. Whenever a communal riot breaks out, there is no *adhān* (call to prayer) or prayer in mosques in that devotees are terrified of moving out of their houses[7].

---

[7] The orgy of violence is predictable: destruction of religious sites, rape of women and mindless killing of innocent children. Worse, victims are hacked to death, pregnant women's wombs are ripped apart and unborn babies are flung to their deaths. Ironically, the perpetrators are emboldened in the name of religion to commit these horrendous deeds under 'fits of hysteria and madness'. Ibid., 4.

The Most Merciful God Does not Approve Corruption in the World

Allah is very sensitive and He does not approve any corruption in the unique world created by Him. It is intolerable for Him that His creation be destroyed. First He warns those guilty of it. If they do not mend their ways, they are eliminated from this world. This is done in order to rule out destruction and to encourage a constructive approach. Such sensitivity is innate also in the human nature. For, no artisan can put with the ransacking of his products. He is bound to take the offender to task. One does not want that anyone should drop any rubbish in his house.

Nadir of Humanity

It is the abyss of decay in our world that we are bent upon destroying everything in the universe. Man is after the blood of other persons. In a trivial scuffle among children of different castes, their parents, rather the entire community gets embroiled. Shedding blood is highly common at the slightest pretext. Can anyone of us reconcile to an attack by a beast on children, and men and women, as a mute spectator? They will defend victims, irrespective of their faith. All people will try their best to control or eliminate that beast in order to save human beings. Given this, why has now man turned into a beast and acts in such a horrible way which may put even beasts to shame?

Noble Souls Appeared in All Eras Instructing Mankind in Godliness and Humanism

Allah warns in the Qur'an: "Do not cause corruption on earth and do not spoil it after it has been set right." (7: 56).

What it signifies is that in every era God has sent down Messengers in order to improve the conduct of people, to establish peace in society to help man recognise his Creator and Lord and to guide mankind to lead a peaceful, decent life. These Messengers directed mankind to the straight way. After them, their successors carried out their message as well - wishers of mankind. They taught Godliness and humanism to people and denounced all forms of mischief, disorder, civil war and all destructive means and ends. They dissuaded people from the wrong course. Such teachers and reformers of mankind have appeared in all eras and in every region. Many such noble souls arrived in India from other parts of the world. They served as spiritual masters, moral teachers, Godly persons and humanists. Some pious souls emerged from the Indian soil too. History bears out their achievements. It is therefore a very serious matter underscoring our ingratitude and insincerity that even in the face of such glorious heritage and centuries-long spiritual and moral reform program we are still liable to indulging in rioting and thus undoing what these noble souls had accomplished.

Sensitivity and Mercy of the Creator and Master of Man and the Universe

The above Qur'anic verse indicates also that Allah takes a strong exception to corruption on earth out of His sensitivity and mercy. He is the Creator of mankind and this universe. Were one to molest or harass the residents of a house, its head is bound to react. For he offended those under his care, thinking that no one will take any action. The master of the house will be full of mercy for the victims who being weak could not defend themselves. Given this, God is most likely to be angry over the recurrent incidents of communal riots, exploitation, barbarity and destructive acts in our country[1]. Let us not forget that He is the Master and Creator of both mankind and this universe.

Violence, Bribery and Mismanagement

Your town is famous for its beauty, greenery and pleasantly moderate climate. It is rightly known as the Garden City. I do not know whether there is a zoological garden here or not. We have got one in Lucknow. If a couple of dangerous tigers or wolves barge in your town and start attacking children and the young and the old, would you put up with it? Would you let them keep attacking everyone? Let me tell you frankly that the two beasts in your midst are violence and corruption. You have left them unbridled. They are no less deadly than beasts. Rather, they have far wider access than that which beasts have. All towns and departments are vitiated by these.

---

[1] This point is pithily expressed in the following words: "The Compassionate and Merciful God Who is even more kind and loving to every man than his own mother, would not be pleased with these acts of wanton destruction. He will not allow this state of affairs to continue for long." These are ominous signs of divine punishment. Nadwi, *The Country on a Dangerous Turn*, 3.

The Most Merciful God Does not Approve Corruption in the World

Two Enemies of the Country

Please remember that if violence is let loose, it does not spare anyone. If you want to save yourselves and this country against destruction, you should be prepared to take on these two dangerous enemies. They are bent on destroying our country Bribery, excessive love of wealth, and violence are now firmly entrenched in our country. They have been eating into our vitals. For the very reason this movement, *Payām i - Insāniyat* has been launched. It seeks to bring Muslims and other brethren on a single platform. It aims at promoting love and harmony among all and to wipe off hatred and hostility. We have observed the signs of the success of our movement everywhere. All countrymen have been responding to our deep concerns. It is the religious duty of Muslims to promote fraternity with all countrymen, to strengthen unity and to allay all misperceptions. They should do all that they can for giving sincere suggestions to the countrymen and to save the country[2]. God will help you in this cause and will protect this country and its residents.

Trend for Violence: A Precursor to Decline and Decay

Let this be borne in mind that violence does not remain confined to any particular community or class. If a group is unable to find an adversary, they turn hostile to one another. Like fire it is a suicidal, self-destructive tendency[3]. The trend for violence on communal grounds in our country will not go unabated. It will engulf everyone. All classes, clans, castes and neighbourhoods will be afflicted by this. This will prove a precursor to the decline and decay of our country.

---

[2] For an elaboration about co-existence between Muslims and other faith groups, see Nadwi, *Islam and Civilisation*, (Lucknow, 1986).
[3] Nadwi points out to binaries of like violence and non-violence that determine the ambience of a country. Nadwi, *Kārwān*, vol.5, 198-9.

Injustice and Barbarity:
The Most Dangerous Disease of Our Society and Country

In the company of friends

We have assembled here today in Lucknow. I would open my speech with a couplet by a leading Urdu poet of Lucknow, Amir Mina'i[1] who is well known to the students of literature and history. This couplet reads thus: "All of my friends are gathered here. Better bare your soul now. For you may not have such company of your friends later." I would cite here also another couplet by Iqbal, the most distinguished poet, philosopher and thinker of the Indian subcontinent[2]. In his Persian couplet he says: "Better wake up. For I cry out of the depths of my heart. Otherwise, one keeps pursuing love, without crying and expressing his anguish. This has been the standard practice."

A Victim's Curse At Times Destroys Everything

Let me humbly state that I am preoccupied with academic work, with my special interest in the comparative study of religions and history, rather universal history. I have studied many books on this subject written in Arabic, Persian, English and Urdu. In the light of my study I have arrived at the conclusion that common to all religions is the belief that injustice is something evil. The Creator of this world does not condone injustice. History tells that injustice has resulted in the downfall of the great empires of the day. It has destroyed flourishing societies and their feats in the academic and literary domains came to a naught.

We learn from history that even an individual victim's curse, woman or man alike, has brought an end to a whole civilisation. Out of sincerity, true sympathy, pragmatism and humanity I must say that a society should not allow injustice, no matter how advanced it might be and what glorious

---

[1] There is a pointed reference to the poetical works of Mina'i (d.1900) in Nadwi's multivolume autobiography.

[2] Muhammad Iqbal (d.1938) was a celebrated poet and philosopher whose impact on Islamic renewal in South Asia in the twentieth century was significant. Nadwi's great admiration for Iqbal may be gleaned from his literary work, *Glory of Iqbal* (Lucknow, 1973).

history it may have. No weak person should be ever crushed. No one should be persecuted. Likewise, no woman should be hurt. No victim should ever curse.

Is Man Alone to be Hunted?

If this meeting hall, what to say of the whole town of Lucknow, is vandalised by someone and if he breaks its furnishing and decoration and attacks those present, would the security staff of this hall let this happen? If you wreak havoc at a potter's shop, he will make life difficult for you. He will deter you from damaging the pots painstakingly made by him. He is bound to retaliate. If you try vandalism at another shop, steal its goods and destroy it by making a show of your power, its owner will not remain a mute spectator. If you cause disorder anywhere, the residents will gather while abandoning their business and forcibly stop you from creating disorder. Next to this meeting hall is a public library which is very dear to me (i.e. Amiruddaulah Public Library, Qaisar Bagh, Lucknow). I greatly value each and every book stacked in it. Were someone to damage its books, which may be easily replaced or reprinted, he would be checked. No one will allow any damage to library books.

Is man alone to be hunted? Are fellow human beings to be killed? Our country exists because of its human population. They hold the key position. Otherwise, it would have been a desolate area. No one goes to a town for hunting, for he knows that every town, be it Lucknow, Ayodhya, Mumbai, Delhi, Ahmadabad or Surat, it is a historic town known as a seat of culture. So one is not allowed to destroy even items made of clay, glass or tin. Since, this is the case, how can anyone even think of killing a human being who has been brought into being by the Creator of this world out His of love, creative power and kindness? Why should a human being be someone's prey? Does man deserve to be hunted like game?

What is to be feared most?

In sum, all religions unanimously declare injustice to be something wicked and evil. Injustice enrages the Creator of the universe. He inflicts unimaginable punishment, calamities, and hardship on those guilty of injustice. God's punishment should make us shudder. As a resident of this country my fate is inextricably tied with the fate of this country, so it is my duty to state that the unjust are bound to be afflicted by divine punishment. Unjust societies and communities are subjected to earthquake, lightning,

Injustice and Barbarity:
The Most Dangerous Disease of our Society and Country

price rise, famine, scarcity of good and epidemic. I need not list more horrible forms of divine scourge.[3]

Thus injustice is something very dreadful. All world religions, cultures, reformers and saints share this consensus view that man is the most precious thing in this world, regardless of his religion, country, clan, ethnicity class, talents and competence or otherwise. Every human being is God's product and represents His creative power and kindness. He is an outstanding masterpiece of God.

Inhuman Behaviour in Various Eras and Countries

A sick person, at times, has fits, related to his nerves and mental order. Both individuals and society are liable to undergo a fit. Even the entire nation might turn hysterical. We know from history that fits of injustice, barbarity have not been peculiar to only individuals. At times these have affected the entire society or country or even era. They take to degrading other human beings. So such behaviour is not surprising or uncommon. However, what is more horrifying is if these fits go unchallenged, with no one to check these. Human civilisation has been at times gripped by cycles of violence and inhumanity. Sometime, the situation turned so grim that is seemed that culture would perish altogether and the human race would become extinct. However, some spirited persons came forward and they changed the course of history. I can cite several such examples on the basis of my in-depth study of history. I would, however, present only two instances in point.

When the Tartars from Turkistan appeared on the scene, it appeared that it would mark the end of the world and nothing will survive. It was assumed that civilisation will have to begin its journey afresh. For the Tartar invasion[4] spelled disaster, including the extirpation of libraries, educational institutions, intellectuals and literate people. Although they hailed from Turkistan in the vicinity of China, even those in Europe dreaded them. Below are some quotations from the works by some leading European historians.

In his celebrated work, *The Decline and Fall of the Roman Empire,* Gibbon

---

[3] Nadwi, *Violence and Tyranny*, 4.

[4] Nadwi critically examines the tragic consequences for the Muslim world in the aftermath of the Tartar invasion during the thirteenth century. He dubs the Tartars as the 'Scourge of God'. See Nadwi, *Saviours of Islamic Spirit,* vol.1, 243- 67.

remarks: "The Swedes learnt from the Russians about the Tartar invasion. They were so terrified that they abandoned their annual routine of hunting on the English coast." In a similar vein H. G. Wells observes: "A political pundit in the early 7th century would have definitely predicted that in the next few centuries the Mongols will establish their rule over the whole of Europe and Asia." Likewise, Harold Lamb opines: "The onslaught by Chengiz Khan hurt the culture and civilisation of the day so badly that half of the world had to re-create a semblance of culture afresh. He reduced to a naught the empires of Khwarizm, Baghdad, Russia and for a short time of Poland."

However, something unexpected happened. Some saints appeared on the scene, interacted with the Tartar chiefs and instructed them in Godliness. They exhorted them to fear God and to have mercy on fellow human beings. By dint of their excellent conduct and morals, spiritual fervour, altruism, sincerity and overflowing love for humanity they won ever the heart and mind of Tartars. The latter were mellowed in their outlook. There are many incidents of this import on record, which cannot be recounted here owing to the constraint of time. These saints were so selfless that we do not know even their names because they made no effort for preserving their names. They, however, managed to convert the semi-civilised Tartars into decent human beings. At a later stage, some good writers, legislators and emperors emerged out of the same primitive Tartars. They preserved culture and civilisation and proved to be the leaders of the world for long.[5]

What is to be feared most?

My thesis is that it is not astonishing to note a community, school of thought, society, country, civilisation or era to fall under the sway of violence and bloodshed.

What is nonetheless horrifying if no group or party comes forward to instruct the wicked ones, to deter them from injustice, bloodshed, to infuse into them love for humanity, sincerity for their country, genuine patriotism and nationalism and concern for the community and country.

Violence as part of life

A student of the philosophy of history, religious teachings, Scriptures, and saints' sayings knows well that man is liable to deviation. Man may fall for

---

[5] Ibid., 258-67.

Injustice and Barbarity:
The Most Dangerous Disease of our Society and Country

wealth, base desires, cynicism, sadism and unnatural gratification. At times, people may not enjoy legitimate forms of entertainment and natural charms and melodious lyrics. They may rather rejoice in killing human beings. Such depravity betrays the nadir of humanity and the lowest abyss of degradation. Yet man does get trapped thus. It has been a recurrent syndrome. A single nation has committed injustice and violence at such a wide scale that even many volumes of history books cannot cover these. People have devised novel ways of enslaving others and of torturing and agonising fellow human beings. All these incidents are recorded in history. It seemed that in the face of such inhumanity, society could no longer flourish. For people had been degraded beyond limit. Women were denied honour.

However, there was a turn of events. Under the welcome influence of spirituality there was a mass movement. People were ready to lay down their lives for a cause. They did not care for their social status, their health and even their life. This led them to overcome fear. Sanity was restored. Those who had turned blood-thirsty regained consciousness. They gave up mindless bloodshed. Rather, they took up the cause of defending everyone. Those notorious for highway robbery were transformed into conscientious security persons.

In hard, bleak times people do not rejoice in their children. The same situation obtains presently in certain parts of our country. People are too worried about their children and grandchildren. They rather cry when they look at their children. For they are concerned about the safety and future of their children. They apprehend that their children may be subjected to a violent death in their own presence by a beastly crowd. What a great pity and shame it is that one may have this acute sense of insecurity about his innocent, smiling children and female members of his family! For in communal frenzy these women and children will undergo inhuman treatment. Even orphans and widows are not spared.[6]

Imperative to raise certain points

Mob lynching stems from perversion.[7] It is patently unnatural. God has not created man for his violent killing. Such frenzy runs counter to the

---

[6] Nadwi, *Violence and Tyranny*, 8-9.

[7] The rising incidence of mob lynching in India is symptomatic of communal frenzy. It features prominently in the ethnic cleansing designs of extremist religious organisations working in collusion with political outfits sharing a similar ideology.

teachings imparted by God's Messengers and reformers. However, mob lynching is a grim reality. Hence it is imperative to discuss it, though with a heavy heart. One feels like crying while reporting it. As an academician I have to write about it. For this is all part of history which will be studied by subsequent generations. They will figure out what kind of persons we were. They will find out about their ethnicity, and their habitat. They will wonder as to why they used to indulge in such mindless violence. For they had behaved so callously, without any sensitivity or tender feeling. They will ask whether these culprits were blind and deaf to every value. Did they never regret what they did? Were they so stone-hearted that they remained a silent spectator to the gory violence all around them? Did they discriminate so much on the grounds of religion and history? They judged others on the basis of some baseless, malicious reports. They used the lens of thousand years old tainted history. While doing all this they disregarded the Ever-Living, Self - Subsisting God.

Man at the Centre of the world

This world owes all of its charms to man. It flourishes because of him only. It is man who produces books and masterpieces and stands out for his intelligence. Man is characterised by tremendous capacity for love. Without man, this world would be worthless. All worldly charms are because of him. One does not enjoy his visit to a graveyard. Nor can one spend his whole life in a museum. A museum houses precious pieces yet one cannot lead life inside it. In contrast, one never grows tired of the human habitat. While crossing an abandoned desolate place he keeps praying for his safety and invokes God for protecting him. He tries to return at the earliest to the human habitation.

Why no protest against man's beastly attitude

If one does not have love, sensitivity and empathy for a fellow human being, he is a wolf, not man. As it is, no one has any good word for a wolf. Rather, everyone hates it. No one gets hurt as a wolf is condemned. In this big crowd facing me, will anyone object to my denunciation of a wolf? Since this is the case, why do not we condemn those persons who behave like a wolf? Why do not we feel hurt when they act? Why do not we disown them? Has man been created to behave as a wolf? On the contrary, man is supposed to emulate an angel or to become a saint. It is man's obligation to be kind and sympathetic to everyone. Man has been exalted to the status of being the best of all creation. This idea features recurrently in our poetry, everyday language, feelings and social gatherings. A wolf stands in contrast

Injustice and Barbarity:
The Most Dangerous Disease of our Society and Country

to man. So, poet has ever glorified it. No sane person has idealised it. We repulse a snake, scorpion, wolf and tiger yet we do not feel ashamed of behaving like these.

Kindness to Human Beings

It is beyond me how one can hit another person. His hand should be medically examined. It should be clinically ascertained as to why he hit someone. For man's hand is not meant for it. Its only purpose is to stop injustice to anyone. We should rescue every human being, be he of Europe, Africa or United States. We must forbid any excess, whether it is committed inside home, in market or anywhere. In his couplet the Urdu poet Hali makes this insightful point: "Man has been created for experiencing and sharing suffering. Otherwise, angels suffice for obedience to God."[8] Prophet Muhammad (peace be upon him) is on record observing: "Allah is kind to those who are kind to people. He is Most Compassionate. Be kind to those on earth. The One in the heavens will be kind to you." The same idea is versified well by Hali in his other couplet. The above hadith is often taught in hadith sessions. Scholars know well the importance of this hadith.

Not to Despair

We need not despair over the present state of affairs. Nonetheless, it is the need of the hour that our religious and political leaders should come forward and exhort everyone to maintain the image and honour of our country. We should not bring disrepute to our own country. We should behave like decent persons and have love for one another. The joy of life consists in loving one another. This mutual love assures one that others will rescue him, if one faces a crisis. Peaceful life for everyone rests on patriotism and peaceful co-existence.

Need for controlling frenzy

Our country is now ravaged by frenzy, madness, sheer emotion and politico-religious exploitation. Let us hope that it is a temporary phase which will be over soon. However, for keeping it under check some persons

---

[8] Nadwi, *Violence and Tyranny*, 10.

should come forward. People should stand up extending sympathy to others and taking care of them. They should work selflessly, without any regard for their own comfort. They should tour across the country in delegations, address people, and appeal to them in the name of country, humanity, reason, justice and God to put an end to religious frenzy. People should be encouraged to channelise their energy into constructive work. They should be asked to devote themselves to progress, nation building and bringing glory to their country. All this will bring prestige to our country. For our country has been stigmatised. History bears it out that our country had not been defamed so much earlier. We had not been in the news for the wrong reasons. We are Indians as well as Hindus and Muslims. We all love India and are proud of its history and civilisation. Muslims have not abandoned their homeland, though they could emigrate anywhere. They are committed to their country. Muslims will not leave their homeland. They should act with courage and confidence. They should fit in with power structures and organise themselves. State should discharge its duties. Likewise, schools and colleges, police and media should perform well their assigned roles.

Setting education, police and media right

If the following three constituents of our country - education, police and media are in order, our society will prosper. Then there will be no major threat to polity. Those gaining education should turn out to be enlightened persons, well-versed in respecting fellow human beings. By the same token, police should be characterised with helping and co-operating with the public. Let me tell you frankly that when abroad, I feel comfortable, if police is around. There the police is regarded as a guide and helper. Once I sought directions from a constable in London and felt too embarrassed. For he gave me not only directions, he also escorted me up to my destination. Police is there to help people, not to commit excess against anyone. The weak and the poor receive their special attention. Let us keep this point in mind that the British being a foreign aggressor in India had set up the Department of Police in order to terrorise Indians.[9] That role of police is now irrelevant. In the independent India we should have felt happy and secure in the presence of police. They are expected to help those in distress, women and children. The general perception of a saviour about police should have been in the public mind. I therefore reiterate my conviction that if education, police

---

[9] The parallel Nadwi draws between British colonialism and the present realities in the subcontinent has a common feature: violation of human dignity.

Injustice and Barbarity:
The Most Dangerous Disease of our Society and Country

and media discharge well their assignments, ours will be a safe, happy country.

No need to panic

We should not be panic-struck on noting the all-round frenzy gripping everyone. After all, man is man. All this is part of life. Life is full of ebb and flow. What is nonetheless a serious issue is the absence of any group coming forward to arrest this epidemic. There should be someone to control disorder. If no organisation, party or just, decent, patriotic, nationalist persons take up this cause, a country cannot be safe and secure, even if it surpasses others in material resources and prosperity. People may have a high standard of life. However, if they do not have peace of mind, their wealth will be of no avail. What is most important is that all countrymen should enjoy mutual love, peace and trust.

It is very odd that we get afraid of other human beings. Beasts, snakes and scorpions are to be dreaded, not fellow human beings. Was man created for killing other men? Does man not have other risks and threats?

Saints and devout persons transformed the Tartars into decent human beings. They learnt to abide by law and preserve culture. This feat was accomplished by spiritual masters. Securing our country's Independence was no easy task. The British Empire then extended far and wide. As a child I had learnt that the sun never sets in the British Empire. For the British rule was spread from one corner of the world to another. It was initially a dream that our country will ever be free. However, patriotic Hindu and Muslim Indians under the leadership of Gandhi, and revered Islamic scholars like Abul Kalam Azad, Muhammad Ali, Shawkat Ali, Abdul Bari Farangi Mahali, Shaykh al-Hind Mahmud al-Hasan, Husayn Ahmad Madani and the political activist Nehru family pledged to boycott the British.[10] Gandhi and Azad were in the forefront of the Freedom movement. Notwithstanding the differences in their culture and language, Hindus and Muslims were united then. In my early years I have seen and listened to the speeches of Gandhi and Motilal Nehru. We had a close family affinity with Azad. These political leaders achieved what was unthinkable. Our country became free. When they had embarked on the Freedom movement, they were dismissed as crazy persons who were living in a fool's paradise. They

---

[10] Nadwi, *Muslims in India,* 115-8.

were taken as abnormal. For driving out the British was then unimaginable. However, by dint of the Hindu-Muslim unity, patriotism and commitment the Indians compelled the British into leaving India.

Secularism, Democracy and Non-Violence

Gandhi and his associates, among whom the most notable one was Azad, presented the following three ideals for the survival, peace, prosperity and happiness of the country: secularism, democracy and non-violence. These are vital for our survival. This truth must be noted and assimilated by all, particularly scholars and historians, that our country cannot flourish without these. Today I reiterate the same that democracy, secularism and non-violence are the key to our success. It is the divine decree that Hindus, Muslims, Jains, Buddhists, Sikhs and Christians will continue to live in this country. It is part of divine dispensation in that they have settled here. Given this, a secular India is the best option.

History cannot be reversed

A pre-Islamic Arab poet points out in his couplet that fire being self-destructive consumes itself, if it does not have anything to burn.[11] I, therefore, warn that if Muslims are marginalised and their holy places are desecrated here, it will lead to internal strife. The Backward classes, Jains and Buddhists will demand the restoration of their places of worship. In eighth century the Shankra Acharaya in south India had turned all Buddhist places of worship into temples. I have witnessed these places. I have been to the Buddhist Nalanda University which has been recently excavated. I have seen also thousands of Jain and Buddhist places of worship turned into temples which are now controlled by Hindus.

I have written letters to all Prime Ministers since the days of Rajiv Gandhi.[12] These letters have been already published. I insist that efforts should not be made to reverse or distort history. We should rather focus on moving forward. Since our life is short and limited, we should not waste it

---

[11] Nadwi, *Kārwān,* vol.5, 98.

[12] An important strategy of Nadwi was to apprise the country's Prime Ministers of the impending dangers and urged them to work for reform and the citizens' welfare. See Bilal Abdul Hayy Hasani, *Sayyid abul Hasan Ali Nadwi: Thought and Mission* (unpublished), 188-200.

on pointless things. Let us make the best use of resources and opportunities for doing something positive. Few persons get a long, ripe age. Given this, we should not waste time anymore. It is foolish to spend our energy, time and talents on such a useless exercise. We should take our country forward. It is the height of foolishness to take our country back into it. If we get entangled into this, we will not have any time for doing something useful. Such waste of time and energy will land us into serious trouble and enervate us. It will bring infamy to our country, leaving a big stigma on its face. This will push our great heroes, thinkers and philosophers into oblivion. Our country will get infamous as a place where innocent people are burnt alive and cut into pieces or thrown into a saw machine. It will be discredited as a place where even small children are thrown out of moving trains.

God does not approve such mindless violence. We may land on the moon and stars. However, as reported by C. M. Joad, the following episode is instructive, rather a matter of pride for all Indians. According to him, when Dr Radha Krishnan, an eminent Indian philosopher called on him, someone told him about the scientific accomplishments in the West, including the landing on the moon, covering long distances between continents in a short time etc. Upon this Dr Radha Krishnan remarked! 'Yes, you now swim like fish in water and fly in air like birds but you still do not know how to live like human beings on earth."[13] Dr Zakir Hussein has quoted this episode. When I was present at the Golden Jubilee celebrations of Jamia Millia Islamia, Dr Zakir Hussein asserted: "The birth of every baby indicates that God has not still given up on man. Otherwise, He would not have sent another human being to this world. However, our own conduct betrays cynicism on this count." (He had made this observation against the backdrop of the frequent incidents of violence in Delhi in 1947). While God has not despaired, we have a deep distrust for human beings.

Man's Trial

Let us test man. For God has gifted him with such a sensitive heart which no other creature possesses. Being well-versed in my religion I dare say that even angels do not share this privilege. Prompted by his heart, man shares others' sorrow, is moved into tears and turns to God fervently crying for His help. Man is therefore to be respected and all human beings be treated

---

[13] A similar view is echoed in Nadwi, *Western Civilisation, Islam and Muslims,* 147.

well because they belong to the same fraternity. Yet we have debased ourselves so much that we thrash and trample upon fellow human beings and target defenceless children and women. The ghastly, inhuman incidents in Mumbai, Ahmadabad and Surat are instances in point. It sends chill down your spine. I have been a frequent traveler. I do not have words to recount as to what happened there. Naked women were made to parade there. Needless to add, they were molested. They were even

shot dead. This does not befit any religion. Zor is it in accord with the norms of humanity, reason, decency or Indian customs and traditions. In the past our country was held in much esteem in view of the great masters born here.

A Menace for Every Culture, Country and Era

In conclusion, let me affirm this important point that the problem confronting us is not very serious. What is nonetheless more worrisome is the absence of any solution to this problem. It agonises me that there is no one to take care of those in distress. Nor is there any concerned person. No one is coming forward to cure the disease. This apathy is a grave danger for any country, culture or era. This world survives only because some persons have concern for humanity and values. The Messengers, sufi masters, noble souls, sympathisers and concerned friends have made life pleasant. They abandoned their own comfort, joys, food and drink, and family for the sake of salvaging humanity, and for protecting fellow human beings against violence and bloodshed. They protested against inhumanity. For this they gave up their food and sleep and risked their own lives. We need today the same dedicated, noble souls.

We expect that the esteemed persons on and off the dais will gather courage to champion this cause. Let us hope that political and religious leaders will join them in putting an end to the present grim situation. Let us ensure that such shameful incidents do not recur. We must strive for eliminating such violence. God is pleased as one worships Him, and serves His servants. The construction of buildings does not please Him. He has already created everything for man. Even the places of worship are for man's use. Animals do not worship there.

I took your precious time, as it was an excellent opportunity to share my innermost feelings with you. For this opportunity may not arise later. We are not sure if we would survive for long or meet you again as you have gathered today in such large numbers. We very much look forward to a positive response to our plea. We hope that some noble souls will rise to the occasion and others will follow them. This will help transform the present

Chapter 11

Injustice and Barbarity:
The Most Dangerous Disease of our Society and Country

deplorable and pitiable conditions of our country. May God grant us the strength to accomplish this feat.

Evil Consequences of Injustice

Mutual Trust: The Axis of Life

Let me first thank you for having assembled here in response to our call. Justice and civility demands that I should express my gratitude to you for your kind gesture. Mutual trust has prompted you to join us at this gathering. Your confidence in us, humanism and patriotism also account for this. You are not here for any fun or entertainment. We have not organised here any tournament or show or recreational event. That you have still assembled here is a healthy sign. As long as we trust one another, it is in the interest of humanity. Mutual trust is the main axis of life. Getting some benefit, intelligence, scholarship or genius alone cannot serve as the basis of life.

The working of our world is premised on mutual confidence, trust and respect. We expect everyone to do good. If we turn cynical and misperceive everyone as opportunist, dishonest, harmful, dreadful like beasts or snakes or scorpions, life cannot go on. In the absence of mutual trust, all of our technology, knowledge and universities would be of no avail. We know that the working of the world has been based since time immemorial on mutual trust, confidence, respect and good expectations.

I cannot suppress the expression of my joy over your presence here in large numbers. I have very old association with your town, Ghazipur. What I gathered from history, family tradition and my studies, Ghazipur stands out as an important place for me. Our family has had links with your town. As a result, I have always felt drawn towards you. For me it is not an alien place in view of my ancestral roots here.

Health and Sickness Being Part of Life

Without any further preliminaries and without being pedantic let me talk to you in a simple, direct way. Both health and sickness are natural states for man. Man is prone to both as these are part of his life. Inanimate objects like a wall or mountain do not fall sick. We are subject to earthquakes and floods. However, that is an altogether different topic. Health and sickness being natural traits should not depress or antagonise us. A sick person does recover. This holds true for not only an individual but for a society as a whole. History bears it out. History is not a record of only conquests, accomplishments and heroic feats. Rather, it presents an amalgam of both rise and fall, justice and inhumanity, and progress and decay, including even self-destruction.

A Sick Society is not Unusual

As an individual falls sick, a society too, is vulnerable to decline and decay. Same applies to even a civilisation or era. At times, the whole age spanning over years was ravaged by decadence. For details one may consult *Historians' History of the World* or *The History of the Decline and Fall of the Roman Empire* or the history of Arabia, Persia and our own country, India. All these civilisations have been afflicted occasionally with decadence. At times, these storms have caused havoc for long. Sometimes a civilisation lay dormant for 100 long years or 50 or 10 years. Its duration depends upon the forces which govern society.

In medical terms, man, at times, undergoes a fit of hysteria. This fit may grip even a nation. However, this too, is part of life and we need not grow despondent. Even the whole civilisation or era may be afflicted by it.

When the Tartars from China and Turkistan set out, as documented in T. W. Arnold's *The Preaching of Islam,* they shook the then entire world. It appeared that if they were not checked for their savagery, and continued to do as they wish, it would spell the end of the world. Mankind will then have to undertake a journey afresh for constructing a new civilisation and for recreating a new order in view of the all-round destruction. Libraries, and educational centres razed to the ground will have to be built again. More importantly, man will have to be purged of the false sense of demonstrating his power, his triumphalism, and his gratification of desires. This is, all the more, disturbing if not an individual, but the whole nation may behave thus. Even the entire era may be carried away by it. According to Arnold, when the Tartars marched forth from China and Turkistan, the fishermen of England and Denmark were so terrified that they did not go out for weeks and months out of their fear of Tartars. Their pillage had shaken the whole world. Everyone felt despondent. For no one could lead life with any degree of peace and satisfaction. Let us remember that mutual trust and confidence is the axis of life. That confidence had been shattered in that people had lost trust in one another. One feared that another person will kill him. The Tartars were so insensitive that they used to erect towers made of their victims' skulls. This was their show of bloodshed, rather massacre. In Baghdad the water of the Tigris rivers turned red on account of the blood of those butchered by the Tartars. On another day, it turned all black owing to the ink of the manuscripts sunk into it. An atmosphere of pessimism

Evil Consequences of Injustice

enveloped everyone.

Yet some noble souls came forward. They won over the hearts of these stone-hearted Tartars and changed their mindset altogether. The Tartars had taken everyone by storm and it appeared that the world was doomed. It was on the brink of extinction. At that juncture these pious persons encountered the Tartars, without resorting to sword. By dint of their virtues, empathy, concern for humanity, overflowing love and respect for fellow human beings they changed the heart and mind of Tartars. The same Tartars abandoned their life of pillage, killing and violence and came to be known as emperors of vast kingdoms and patrons of culture and civilisation. Otherwise, they would have spent all their life in killing and bloodshed. Among them some attained fame as men of letters and saints.

God's Messengers Catering to Everyone

In my opinion the vulnerability of an individual, a locality, a town, a country or even an era to violence is not unusual. History is littered with such examples. Nothing much is left in history if we excise such instances. Messengers of Allah and their reform missions, devout and pious persons and saints appeared on the scene to curb these bouts of violence. During intervals in history, abnormal conditions prevailed, calling for the advent of noble souls. They did shoulder this responsibility and took good care of the whole community. Reformers and saints oversaw the moral reform and progress of their respective societies and countries.

A Big Danger

There is hope as long as there are pious souls around us who reject evil, injustice and disorder. They grow restless on noting any degeneration. However, if such custodians are not there, it will be something disturbing. If we fail to identify them or look for them, while they are located in some remote spot, hundreds of miles away, it spells a big danger.

As rightly pointed out by Professor Anees Chishti, the big danger lying ahead of our country, India is that such committed, noble souls are nowhere to be seen. There is no one who feels concerned over such outrageous incidents. No one abandons his food and drink for this cause. Nor does anyone feel the urgency to come out, proclaiming that they would protect the country from disorder and destruction. We believe that God has created all of us. Given this how will God reconcile to this destruction? In this context I often use the example of a petty potter who would not put up at all, if someone were to destroy his pots. He would challenge and resist, and ask as to how one dared to harm him and destroy his products which entailed hard work for him. So, will God, the Creator of all, tolerate the sacrilege of His creation? Are we authorised to kill thousands of human beings created by Him, like a trivial object?

Is God not at all concerned?

Let us see reason. If someone barges in this assembly hall and overturns chairs no one will allow this. Since man feels so much concerned about his possessions, will God allow us to put to death those created by Him out of love? A student of medicine and anatomy, rather even an ordinary person knows well that God protects well the foetus in the mother's womb.

He ensures that the baby is placed properly and securely, with his/ her own faculties of breathing, seeing, hearing and thinking and its delivery as the newly born baby at the appointed time. Had God not devised the whole arrangement, a baby could not come out of his/her mother's womb. Nor could the baby express himself/herself after being born. It is God Who protects the baby all along. Parents take every care of the child. Under God's protection every child grows. Again, it is He Who enables the child to move and grow. Given this, no one has a right to kill him when he comes of age. Do we not at all fear God, our Creator? How can we dare destroy God's own creation?

If one tries to demolish someone's house or fell anyone's tree, he will not be allowed to do so. Likewise, God will not reconcile with the mass killing of human beings. Things cannot go on thus.

At times, I make this remark that as father returns from a long journey or even work and when his children and grandchildren throng him, he should rejoice. However, he looks worried and disturbed. On being asked if he was feeling all right, he tells that he is fine. However, this horrible thought troubles him that if a communal riot erupts, his near and dear ones will be mercilessly killed liked insects and harmful animals. This agonises him. May God have mercy on all of us! I do feel concerned about this father.

I read newspaper reports, hear accounts and have even witnessed firsthand that in communal riots even children and women are not spared. This is patently abnormal and unnatural and inimical to the human nature. It runs contrary to God's mercy and justice. He is very much concerned about His creation. Why do we forget this? Can He tolerate the destruction of His creation? Such a country can never prosper.

Studying history is my passion. I have noted this in history that as darkness loomed over mankind, a noble soul appeared on the centre stage. He sacrificed himself for the sake of humanity. This put humanity on the right track, as it got a new lease of life. Such saints were born in our country as well, who had overflowing love for mankind and devoted their lives to bridging gaps among human beings.

Invaluable Role Models

Let me present an instance in point. Farid al-din Ganj i -Shakar was a noted sufi master. Someone gave him a knife as a present, as it was a famous product of handicraft. He thought that it will be of much use in his spiritual lodge (*khanqah*) for cutting fruits and vegetables. However, far from being pleased over this present, the saint quipped: "This knife is of no use for me. I prefer a needle which joins things together, not a knife which tears things apart. My mission is to console and join the broken hearts. You should have better presented a needle to me."

His successor, Nizām al-din Awliyā was committed in an equal degree to the love for humanity. Our country should be proud of such noble souls. His shrine is in Delhi and is held in esteem by everyone. During his lifetime, his devotees used to bring for him presents such as sweets and fruits which he would distribute among the poor. He used to fast consecutively throughout his life. In accord with the shari'ah, however, he did not fast only on the two Eid days. Otherwise, on all days in winter and summer he observed fasting. Many packed presents having sweets and other gifts reached him daily.

Someone thought that the shaykh did not know anything about the packed presents. For he used to direct his servant, Iqbal to distribute everything among the children of those staying in his *khanqah*. So that person packed some dust and presented it in a gift pack to the shaykh. He believed that as usual the shaykh would think that some sweets are inside it. That had planned it as a test for the shaykh. When Iqbal was about to pick that packet along with other presents, the shaykh directed him to leave that packet with him. He told Iqbal that it contained kohl which he would apply to his eyes. That person who was watching all this fell on his knees, requesting forgiveness for his disrespect to the shaykh. Such was the mercy, generosity and nobility of these saints.

Some Committed Persons Should Come Forward

What is amiss in our country presently is that everyone is engaged in their business. There is no element or group in our society which protests against the injustice rife in our midst. I do not say that all are inclined towards injustice. As to those who are present in this meeting, I can affirm with certainty that they hate injustice. It is the need of the hour that some pious souls should appear, publicly declaring that they will not let any of this misdeed happening and an Indian killing another Indian, bribery or usurpation. I respect government, no matter who is in power. The state and its administrative staff are to be respected. However, what is needed is a robust, public conscience, repulsing evil, appreciating virtue, and denouncing evil and injustice. If this consciousness is not deeply rooted, our country cannot flourish.

I am not someone to forecast as I am not a spiritual master. However, as a devoted student of history I tell this with utmost conviction that a country, notwithstanding its amazing achievements in the domains of science, technology, literature and even nuclear energy cannot survive, if it does not profess and practise justice, mercy, humanism, revulsion towards evil and appreciation of good.

This is what has inspired us to approach and address you. We do not have any means or organisation. By God's grace, however, we have some Hindu brethren as friends, whom Anees Chisti named in his speech. In addition, we have some other supporters. We have been across the country, having visited several states, including their capitals, ranging from Mumbai to Himachal Pradesh, and from Kolkata to south India. We have tried to reach wherever we could. We have always insisted on this point that we have not despaired of man. Man is after all man. His conscience has been clouded for the time being. However, he is gifted with a living heart, a thinking mind and a vibrant conscience.

Let us have concern for the whole country

What has brought us to your town is to convey this important message: Please have concern not only for your own town, but also for your state and the whole country. Please ensure that nothing inhuman or barbaric happens. For a country cannot last for long if injustice is rife there. Or a calamity may overtake it, in the form of earthquake, flood, drought or outbreak of epidemics. God warns us in a variety of ways. Before this stage is reached, we should mend our ways. Let us rejoice in the happiness of others. We should not discriminate among people on the basis of their religion, saying that one is a Muslim and the other a Hindu or a Christian. Rather, we should accept everyone as a human being. We all are part of the same fraternity, being the members of the human race, as citizens of India, and as residents of the same state. Above all, we all are the creatures of God. We are part of the

Evil Consequences of Injustice

same family, same clan and same fraternity. Hence, we are brethren to one another.

There have been many noble souls in our country and elsewhere also who risked their own lives in order to protect others. This nobility accounts for the perpetuity of the human race. Without this virtue the human race would have been extinct by now. There have been numerous attacks and plans for genocide in the world which could obliterate the human race. However, humanity has thrived owing to such pious souls. I have already cited the example of the Tartars. I may provide some more instances, illustrating how some altruistic servants of God revived the spirit of humanity and awoke people to truth. They recharged the dormant spirit of man and renewed conscience. They did not stoke hatred and hostility. Rather, they promoted friendship. And they exhorted all sincere well- wishers. Their audience grasped their message and shunned injustice. Then the same people were able to erect vast empires, promote knowledge and set up libraries. As a result, culture and civilisation flourished and mankind survived. So the entire region of Iran, Turkistan and Afghanistan which adjoins our country was salvaged.

Let us save our country against destruction

You are free to do your own business in line with your interest and competence. Your tastes and roles are most welcome. However, all of you must resolve to save your country against destruction. For self - destruction is not to the liking of God, our Creator. He does not approve the killing of man by another man. He will not put up for long with this horrid practice. Man may be attacked by a snake or a wolf or any other beast lurking in the forest. It is, however, beyond logic that man may stoop to the level of a beast or behave like a deadly snake or scorpion. It defies logic and common sense.

We have neglected this important reality in our country. This has pushed us further into backwardness. Our intense desire for political power and the mode of election have been our bane. In election we raise such slogans which suit people and prompt them to vote for us. We try to woo our own clan and community. At that stage we do not tell that we would crush other communities. We focus on getting votes by our own community. This system cannot last for long. For it is discordant with civility.

Saving the country in our own different ways

Since all of you are busy, educated persons, you may have formed an idea about our mission. Your efforts for reform should not be confined to your town alone. While taking note of your potentials and strength and utilising your contacts and your free time, you should stand against the present trend for genocide, communal riots and corruption. The root cause of our malaise is our lust for money. We may stoop to any level for the sake of money. It is a fatal attraction and a deadly poison that is bound to kill and destroy the human race, our civilisation and ordinary civil life. With this obsession, children cannot focus on study and workers cannot perform duty properly. It deprives us of our peace of mind, leaving us restless day and night.

In the past Hindus and Muslims had excellent cordial relations. I have seen the wedding cards in Urdu sent by our Hindu brothers to Muslims, inviting them to the auspicious ceremony. They used to live together. In my childhood I saw that everyone interacted, without any distinction of religion. They would help one another. In a crisis everyone gathered, Hindu and Muslims alike, for help. This was true of every village and town. Our country was known for such unity. I have been to almost all countries in the world and a frequent traveler to the UK. Almost every year I am in the UK, US and have visited France, Belgium, Germany, Switzerland and Spain. I testify before you that our country was acclaimed there for Gandhi who had served well his country out of his love for it. He risked his own life in order to uphold the interests of his countrymen. His committed associates, Nehru and Azad strove hard for freeing their country. After Independence they tried their best to protect it and to carve out a place for it in the comity of nations.

We are inheritors of this glorious legacy. At least we should convey their message to our family, neighbours, especially children and try to change their mindset. The media spreads poison. Our press has turned rabidly communal. Other forums too, fan mutual hatred and provoke people's sentiments. If we disapprove their nefarious designs, they will mend their ways. They only seek popularity. If you do not like their stance, this trend will be changed.

Your town, Ghazipur has to its credit its glorious history. As I explained to you, Sayyid Ahmad Shahid was the first to stand against the British. He appealed to the Maharajah of Gwalior for help against expelling the British mercenaries who had taken over India. Please bring to mind that Sayyid Ahmad lived in Rae Bareli, U.P. yet he sought help from such a far-off place as Gwalior. He proposed that together they should drive out the British. After this they will decide about the regions to be ruled between them and the posts to be allotted respectively. This was the first letter written out of patriotic fervour. Tipu Sultan too, had a close link with the family of Sayyid Ahmad. Tipu fought relentlessly against the British. At his martyrdom, the British commander- in- chief made it a point to inspect Tipu's dead body and remarked: "Now onwards India is ours." He felt mightily relieved and assured over Tipu's death. For he knew that no one else could challenge the British. In sum, Hindus and Muslims participated in an equal degree in the struggle for Independence.

Likewise, together we should now strive for protecting and saving our country. We should identify the evils around us. Similarly, we should be alert about injustice and develop brotherhood. I do not want to tax you any further. I am grateful to the conveners of this meeting and to you for having spared your time. You did not know the speakers at this meeting. Yet, out of your humanism and nobility you assembled in such large numbers. This is a source of tremendous inspiration and strength for us. May God shower more courage upon us! May He enable to save our country!

Self – Destruction

We should not drag religion or other considerations of caste and clan in everyday life. Once we think along religious lines, we are liable to be divided also according to the labels of caste and clan. I had recited an Arabic couplet to the then Prime Minister, V. P. Singh when he met me in Rae Bareli and Lucknow. This couplet makes it plain that when fire has nothing to burn, it consumes itself. He told me that he would quote my observation. He remembered well my comment that if there is no fuel, fire eats itself, for it is self - destructive by nature.

If we allow discrimination on religious grounds and this bias seeps into our mindset, it will lead to further divisions. For, at a later date we will think of partiality on the grounds of caste, clan, family, colour, culture, individual and collective lifestyle. In that eventuality our country will be reduced to a battlefield.

This is not mere speculation. This affliction has seized certain countries which are now lost into oblivion. Many cultures, civilisations and empires were trapped by the same menace. On reading world history one notes only their traces, as they have vanished. They were obliterated because of in-fighting and civil wars. Killing turned out to be their hobby. Out of a false sense of grandeur they would kill anyone and everyone. This tendency for violence overtook them so much that they killed the members of their own clan, family and even their brothers.

So we must put an end to violence, injustice, cruelty, bloodshed, and humiliation. While shedding someone's blood is the ultimate crime, even degrading and enslaving anyone for one's own prestige is a serious disease. Same holds true in the mad race for grabbing wealth. This menace overpowers not only individuals, but also cultures, nations and civilisations. Even religions are not immune to it. One carried away by this menace focuses only upon his interest. He pursues this goal blindly while disregarding others' plight. He turns blind to others' degradation and even killing. For his only target is to amass more and more money, a higher bank balance, name and fame, ministry and political power. This results in a confrontation between political parties and communities. This clash of interest saps life of its joys. Life turns into a battlefield. There was an interval between the two World Wars. However, if now another great war erupts, it will be unending in that it will destroy everyone. Let us realise this big danger. This danger will not affect only the minority community; it will encompass the whole country. This poses a challenge to normal conditions, man's confidence and co-operation. Man will find himself in wilderness or in a museum. He will be surrounded then by beasts alone.

Life does not consist in only eating and drinking

Let us realise that the joys of life are not confined to eating and drinking. At times, facing hunger is more joyful than having a full belly. There have been many noble souls belonging to various religions who preferred starving to eating, and who gave the food of their family to others. Our country too, witnessed such incidents. These values sustain religions, civilisations and the human race. Had it not been so, the human race would have been extinct by now. Like other creatures, man too, would have vanished from the planet earth.

So, we all should maintain and promote normalcy, mutual confidence and love and goodwill for everyone, irrespective of their religion, nationality or linguistic group. We should take him as a member of our fraternity, whether he belongs to our town or country or not. We should have concern for everyone, for he is a human being and hence one of our brethren. We have ties of kinship, both close and distant ones. We may have our close relatives in such far-off countries as Arabia, Iran, England or US.

Songs of Love

Our country enjoys the distinction of having promoted the songs of love which feature in ancient literature, poetry and history. One may read these songs for enjoyment even today. These present the message of fraternity, urging that one should love everyone, have sympathy with them, feed them while denying food to oneself. Such bonds of fraternity have been our distinctive feature. If we do not preserve this tradition, opportunism will overtake us. We will then miss these expressions of love. We appreciate a person who addresses us with respect and love. Likewise, we like the ties of kinship and meeting others. If we are not careful, these life-enriching traditions will disappear forever. We should make efforts in this direction. This is what has brought me here. Otherwise, I had many other preoccupations of academic work, membership of learned societies and chairmanship of various organisations. However, if our own country, our homeland, our neighbourhood and our own homes are not in order, one will not enjoy his trip abroad or the historic tourist spots there. In the absence of peace, tranquility, mutual confidence and trust, at home or in one's country, one cannot enjoy life anywhere.

So our concern is the welfare of our country. At this ripe age I would not have traveled. Moreover, addressing public meetings is not to my taste. I would have continued my academic pursuits. However, God has gifted us with conscience. If conditions are not normal in our country, nothing will work. Likewise, if we lack peace and order and mutual respect and confidence, one cannot carry out any academic work or overseas trip. One would not enjoy even a family wedding party. If we do not have ties of fraternity, and humanity or of nationalism, it is a serious matter. Moreover, we should always bear in mind that we all are creatures of the same God.

How can man attack another man?

We have not ever seen a group of snakes attacking another group of their species. Though I have been a hunter, I never witnessed a pack of wolves killing another pack. Same is true of other beasts. This savage killing of one's own species is not part of the animal life. Given this, it is beyond logic how man attacks another fellow human being. Is man worse than snakes or scorpions? It is something downright shameful. We inhabit the same country and live and die in the same land yet we act as enemy to one another. As to Muslims, those who opted for Pakistan left a long time ago. We also had offers with incentives to emigrate to Pakistan. We, however, turned down those offers, affirming that we have been born in India and it is our home country. We have resolved to stay here. Even in the face of such resolutions, if we are unable to live together peacefully, it is nothing short of a tragedy. It is indeed an ordeal.

We have issued this call out of the same concern. We may have a small audience but we are committed to this call. History testifies that a mission does not fail. Whenever a call is made, it does have some impact. It may be that only a few may respond positively. Yet we know from history that at times only a handful of persons have been successful in changing the course of history. Even a microscopic minority group has sometimes transformed a country by way of directing the majority to the straight way.

Both the means and ends should be pious

We have approached you with the same positive expectation. We will make the same call wherever go by God's help and support. We look forward to your positive response. People should come forward in every town. This will go a long way in protecting your town against infamy and in averting civil war. We should dissuade people from their craze for name, fame and wealth and lust for materialism.

If we behave badly, the integrity of our country will be at risk. Even if a nation survives, it will carry a stigma. Indians will be singled out abroad, in the UK, and US for their indulgence in in-fighting and communal riots. This does not augur well for our country. So far our country has enjoyed goodwill. The contributions of Gandhi and his associates, namely Azad and Nehru who led the Freedom movement, are cited abroad as role models. Let us maintain the prestige and glory of our country. We should uphold this goodwill and trust. Let us behave decently. Triggering communal and caste riots is a ploy for grabbing political power. The vested interests employ even unfair means for meeting their ends. Using unfair means for achieving a target is something wrong. Both the means and ends should be pious. This is the essential teaching of all religions, moral codes, saints, and of our Freedom fighters and national leaders.

In conclusion, I thank you for your attentive listening to someone whom you did not know beforehand. You listened to me patiently. May God shower upon you success and help you realise your noble objectives.

Concern for the Protection and Survival of Humanity

Something Astonishing

I am gratified to meet such worthy persons as you. I am never after big crowds in my meetings. There may be a few listeners but they should have commitment to this cause, concern for humanity, and abounding in sincerity and self-sacrifice. For this is what we want. History bears it out that only a few have always brought about a revolution. I am therefore pleased to note this small but select gathering of committed persons who grasp the issues well.

A father is naturally grieved over his son's illness. Let us have the same intensity of sorrow over the sickness of our neighbour, a resident of our town and anyone in the country. Once again, history testifies it and I affirm this as a student of history that when such noble and pious feelings permeate us and we possess a sensitive heart, it is bound to transform our society. It can improve our society. It can bring happiness and glory to one's family and country. However, this change is effected by only those pious persons who are free from bias and who are willing to lay down their lives for the protection and survival of humanity. They defend humanity at all costs. It is a pity that the scene has changed now. There is an unnatural trend now. That man should dread fellow human beings is something shocking. Man's fear of beasts is understandable. But why should man fear another person? This scenario is horrible and poses a threat to man's survival[1].

Our Responsibility

Let us all resolve to ensure peace in our country. We should not bring any disgrace to its prestige and fair name. The way out is to live cordially. We should not look down upon anyone. Such mean thoughts should not even cross our mind. Our country is famous for its tradition of mutual love and co-existence. Even now it enjoys the same reputation. As a frequent traveler to Europe and the US. I have observed firsthand this positive image of our country. People abroad receive us warmly on learning that we are from

---

[1] The speech in essence captures the mission of the *Payām* movement: human dignity transcends the barriers of race, language and colour. Therefore, self-introspection and commitment to moral regeneration are essential to carry out this universal ideal.

India. For they perceive it as a land of peace and joy.

This image can continue only when we maintain ties of fraternity. We should stop the tendency of looking contemptuously at others. If we do not do so, we will do a great disservice to our country. Rather, we would be traitors to ourselves.

If we do not maintain peace and order, let me candidly warn you that we run a serious risk. Remember that history does not spare anyone. You may read the history of the great Roman Empire. While having meals they needed light and for this they used to burn people alive. They would dine in the light emitted by the bodies set ablaze. They would crack jokes and have fun. Likewise, they would arrange for a fight between a wolf and a human being and watched this bloody encounter with amusement. Gibbon has documented many such incidents in his *Decline and Fall of the Roman Empire*. Those interested in the above subject should read his book. Almost similar reports feature in the works on the decline of the Persian Empire. This mindset has reached our country as well. The tendency to look down upon others afflicts us too. Same holds true for Europe and other developed countries which do not abide by any moral code. They suffer from megalomania. They are liable to face decline. The signs of their fall have been becoming increasingly evident.

Decline notwithstanding progress

Even after the Independence of our country we do not have national unity. There is no doubt the display of efficient machines around us. However, the machine of fraternity, equality, love, sympathy and selfless help for others is not in working order. If despite all progress, we cannot enjoy the fruits of unity and fraternity, it betrays sheer decline in our life. Iqbal, the acclaimed Urdu poet, remarks in his pithy couplets: "What a pity! Man can soar up to the stars yet he cannot control his thoughts. Lost in the matrix of intelligence he cannot decide as to what is beneficial or harmful for him. Though he can harness the rays of the sun, he is unable to light his own life."

Prophet Muhammad (peace be upon him) did not possess any material resources yet he transformed the world with his egalitarian message[2]. On studying history one can grasp better the truth of his message.

Let me place it on record that our country excels others in having produced a higher number of noble souls. While studying their splendid biographies

---

[2] Nadwi, *Islam and Civilisation,* 19-28.

Concern for the Protection and survival of Humanity

one notes the components of nation building[3]. They gave many sacrifices for the development of our country.

Need of the Hour

We should be imbued with sincerity of purpose and love of truth. The need of the hour is to advance in morals, to interact with others in the true spirit of fraternity, without any discrimination and to promote humanistic values. Without this we cannot achieve progress in the real sense. If we survive, we can help others as well. We can lead others only when we purge ourselves of bias and promote mutual social relations, cordial links and love and friendship. I expect you to come forward with a renewed commitment for protecting our country, and for sharing the concern to work in the larger interests of our country while gathering at a single platform.

---

[3] According to Nadwi, nation building rests on three Constitutional pillars: democracy, secularism and non-violence. This position is coherently articulated in his writings in view of India's diverse population and cultures.

What Humanity Needs Most

Allah has brought man into being in this world so that he may lead life. Accordingly, He has provided in plenty all the things which he needs. We all know what are man's basic needs and how these have been provided. Those studying this issue deeply realise that Allah provided for even those things which man needed at a much later stage. These existed even when the world was created. For meeting human needs, He endowed man with the ability and devotion to manage and develop every facet of life. He caused the birth of such groups and individuals who hold their respective professions dearer than even their children. Some of the professions are indeed hazardous. Regardless of the situation, those interested in these professions love them. In this lies the secret of the working of the world. Notwithstanding numerous challenges, every profession has been always advanced.

Food for Thought

Man should reflect on this important issue. Has Allah made any arrangement enabling him to lead his life in accordance with His will, and for guiding him to the purpose and destination of his life? Did this most important issue receive the attention of any group in this world? Who are those who realise the noble purpose of life? Who put their life at stake for accomplishing this important mission?

It runs counter to Allah's mercy that He may not have made any provision for man's essential need. We find around us much wisdom, talent and compatibility with various disciplines of life and we take much pride in them. Given this, even an ordinary person will not accept that Allah may not have instructed man in the purpose of his life and how he can win Allah's pleasure. Allah did send down a series of altruistic persons to meet this basic need. Throughout history they kept guiding mankind how to lead life. They taught man that he should be obedient to Allah in leading life, and that human life is far superior to the animal existence. Man thus holds an exalted position.

Journey of Life

We have in place all sorts of arrangements for driving vehicles and for undertaking a routine journey. Is the journey of life itself not very important? I do not agree that such a crucial journey can be undertaken without the help of any individual or group. For this journey is riven with dangers, rivalry and clashes. Greed may overtake us. We may be cautious about snakes, scorpions, fire and thorns on the way. However, these dangers in the journey of life are fatal. Out of His special mercy and grace Allah devised a system for protecting man against these dangers. In every era He sent down His noble servants who introduced man to his Master and Lord. They showed man the way to his abiding success and welfare. Had this arrangement not been in place, there would have been hardly any difference between man and animals. It was divine dispensation that life should be led at a particular level. So, He brought into being such noble persons who performed this duty. He infused into them such sincerity and commitment that they sacrificed even what was most dear to them for the sake of guiding fellow human beings.

The Final Messenger, Prophet Muhammad (peace be upon him) and character building

Of the Messengers of Allah, Prophet Muhammad (peace be upon him) is the last one. He trained a community, not built on the basis of caste, colour or culture. His call was not restricted to any particular nation, group or country. Rather, he addressed the whole mankind. He asked those to rally around him who would prefer contentment to greed, altruism to selfishness and devotion to Allah, rather than to the base self. Their purpose of life was not to lead life like insects or to devour others like the birds of prey. Rather, through their role model they reminded mankind of their exalted status and the true purpose of their life. They taught fellow human beings that they are Allah's vicegerent, and trustees in this world. Allah has ordained for them greater heights which transcend this limited world[1].

When the final Messenger, Prophet Muhammad (peace be upon him) arrived on the scene, there were countries, nations and empires. It was clear that no one expressed concern to think of humanity. Everyone thought of only himself and his children. People had imbibed animal traits. They raised their own children. Yet they were ever ready to devour others. Among the millions

---

[1] Nadwi, *Islam and the World,* 53-4.

What Humanity Needs Most

of people there was not a single soul who realised the seriousness of the matter. People had no idea of the purpose of their life. The world was like a market, full of consumers. Humanity was at its nadir. Yet even the leading sages, philosophers and poets had no regard for the impending danger.

For changing people's mindset Prophet Muhammad (peace be upon him) raised a band of his followers who were endowed with faith, resolve, action and preaching. They were determined to save mankind from destruction. He trained such selfless and self-sacrificing persons who were more than willing to guide mankind. They had resolved to change the course of life and challenge evil. They wanted to put mankind on the straight way. The Muslim community deemed it as its duty to invite people to Allah's way and to guide them. At this crucial juncture Prophet Muhammad (peace be upon him) spurned all the worldly offers which could accrue to him: honour, pleasures of the flesh and the highest position. He set before himself the goal of a bright future for mankind and a purposive life. He presented before mankind a new way of life, premised on certain principles. Those who accepted his call did not do so only verbally or as a set of ritual. It was not the Prophet's mission. The Qur'an bears it out that his call was not confined to personal beliefs and actions. Rather, his followers had displayed in their word and action that they would expend all of their energy, talent and all that was dear to them for forbidding evil and for promoting good in the world. They were to guide the future generations as well. Not only did they explain the difference between good and evil, they also resolved to make piety prevail over evil. They were determined to eliminate Godlessness and lust for base desires. They opened a strong front against evil, injustice, worship of the self and Godlessness. It was their commitment to wage this battle until their last breath. They resorted to all means for eliminating evil and for establishing truth in the world. They had pledged to sacrifice all of their comfort, joys and honour for achieving this goal.

Faith, Action and Preaching

Faith alone cannot transform the world. Even if it is supplemented with action, it cannot curb evil. The mission of Islam consists in faith, action and preaching. Prophet Muhammad (peace be upon him) presented the same model which alone ensures deliverance. Today this blending is rare.

Such faith is needed which is reflected in one's life and which resists opposing forces. Such actions are required which may influence the world.

We do not see any call in the East or West against Godlessness. Today we need to revive the Prophet's model which is an amalgam of faith, action and preaching. It is the biggest need of the hour. The Messengers of Allah presented before us perfect dogma, sound action and altruistic call. On its basis the Muslim community came into existence.

Today if some people have faith, they lack action. Even if they do some acts, they do not preach. Some, no doubt, carry out preaching but they do not have faith and actions to their credit. There are only campaigns, writings and speeches. People's belief in Allah has shrunk. All the calls are only for the betterment of one's own self and children, and, at most, of one's community and country. No one is concerned about humanity, taking it up as a serious issue. There is no one inviting people to lead a faith- based, pious way of life. Who is in anguish over the plight of mankind? People are worried about their health issues, loss of political power or the problems confronting their country. We keenly look for anyone addressing the real issue. We have read with expectations convocation addresses and philosophers' lectures and writings. Much to our disappointment, we noted that they never talk about humanity, belief in Allah and the Afterlife. No one criticises the present wicked way of life. Nor does anyone preach about morals and God-consciousness[2].

We tell Muslims in particular that their present way of life is not in accord with their glorious history, their claims and their articles of faith. They should immediately realise the purpose of their life. Even the biggest industrial towns, factories and material progress cannot avert the disaster which stares the world in the face. Muslims have disregarded their obligation. They have adopted the same way of life which is followed by the communities who do not care about Allah. What mankind needs today is that Muslims should present their model of faith, actions and sincere call. If they do so, people would rush towards them. Their model can resolve the present crisis. They should recognise their role. They should tell people to come out of the morass of worldliness. People should not have such low self-esteem or pursue a self-destructive way of life. I urge my countrymen and friends that plans are chalked out presently for every domain of life. Why do not we care about the purpose of our life? Does it not need our attention? There is no organised campaign in the country for this purpose. In contrast, there are temptations, self-destructive ways, immorality, anti-humanity measures and gratification of the base self everywhere. Sadly, there is no exhortation for encouraging virtues among people, for leading a purposive

---

2 Nadwi, *Basis of a New Social Order,* 19-20.

life and for developing faith and good character.

The Biggest Service

I urge Muslims that if they make a call characterised by sincerity, sympathy and selflessness, people will definitely respond. Love does not need any recommendation. It is something natural. Truth always makes its way. Muslims should present the way of life which is the elixir for mankind. Prophet Muhammad (peace be upon him) had assigned this role to the Muslim community. Whoever takes up this cause will win huge acclaim. It is the biggest service to mankind and our only objective to offer before mankind Prophet Muhammad's role model. Let us make his call the purpose of our life.

Higher Moral Values

A Parable

In my childhood I had heard this parable: Someone was looking for something on a street. On being asked he told that he had dropped a gold coin. Those present tried to help him in his search. When someone pointedly asked as to where he had dropped it, he told that he had lost it inside his house. Since there was no light there, he was looking for it on the well-lit street.

Man's complacency

The above may seem a funny story or joke to you. However, it is a bitter truth. What we have lost, we look for it elsewhere. We search for it at other, unrelated places. This is true of committees and meetings. Peace, tranquility and happiness are related to our inner being. We cannot look for these in the outside world. Humanity has been afflicted from within. We take cosmetic steps to reform it. We need inner peace and joy. We require the ambience of love, sympathy and morals. It is a bitter truth that we lack the very essence of humanity which is our most precious asset. Our hearts are empty and deserted. These are filled with darkness. We look for peace and happiness outside. We have wronged ourselves by sealing off our hearts. This is the scenario across the world. Our hearts have turned bleak, covered by pitch black darkness. We cannot discern anything. Complacency is innate in the human nature. We do not take steps to introspect in order to look for this precious loss. We are interested more in the outside world. We are at a loss now. Even the best minds are unable to identify where we have lost our asset. We focus on gaining information. Since mental activity is easier than introspection, we are more concerned about intellectual pursuits.

Today all are engaged in mental work. No one tries to gain access to the heart. There is no reform possible until humanity returns to basics. If there is darkness, we will have to arrange for light. We will have to search for what we have lost. Without this, life will come to an end. We will be left clueless.

Inescapable Realities

There is a need now for underscoring truth and for instructing man in the purpose of his life. This could improve mutual relations and man could rise above his animal instincts. It could promote mutual love and prompt self-sacrifice. We could develop the sense of fraternity and put an end to mutual hostility. We would have been blessed with mutual trust and love. Unfortunately, we lost sight of truth. We no longer affirm that there is a Creator of this vast universe. Life can be smooth only if it is led in accordance with the will and guidance of the Creator. However, if we revolt against Him and refuse to abide by His directives, there will be sheer chaos. Take for instance a watch. Only a watchmaker versed in its functioning can repair a defective watch. No scholar, however bright and intelligent can repair a faulty watch. One's intelligence alone is not sufficient. Only an experienced specialist can repair it. Likewise, the world would be on the right track, only after following the Creator's directions. We cannot turn blind to these realities. We will have to take these into our stride.

Man as a trustee in this world

Let me talk frankly with you. Accursed is he who cannot speak truth. Today everyone thinks first of his own interest and has little regard for truth or falsehood. Such people cannot reform mankind. Only truthful persons are the asset of this world. They sacrifice their lives for truth.

All the brightness and positive features in today's world are on account of the persons trained by the Messengers of Allah. Their Companions devoted their lives for serving and improving humanity. This is how we inherited our precious legacy. Their way is the only path to salvation. It is a bright way of life shown by them. Let us imbibe this truth that this world is for us and we are for Allah. We should realise our role as a trustee. Likewise, we should have a clear idea about our accountability to Him. If we do not do so, the plight of mankind will not be over. This way of life is no doubt painful. However, this is the only way out. It is a pity that mankind shirked this responsibility and devoted their time and energy to culture and civilisation.

Higher Moral Values

The Problem of Humanity in History

All cultures and civilisations are worthy of respect. The Indian culture is very dear to us. It is our legacy, of which we are proud[1]. In this regard, mankind cannot attain reform by replicating old civilisations. For these are out of date and dead, without anything to offer. They have completed their mission and played their part. Some of their aspects are no doubt quite appealing. But these are not formidable enough to take humanity to great heights and to check the all-round moral degeneration. They do not have any inspiring message for mankind. We cannot plant these elsewhere. A two thousand years old culture is irrelevant now. The ancient civilisations of Arabia, Rome and Greece were mighty and glorious. They have now lost their charm. They are now confined only to archives.

The nexus between humanity and civilization

Humanity is above and beyond a civilisatio. It does not give rise to humanity. Humanity is not particular to time and place. Civilisations are like a dress for mankind, which keeps changing. Man dresses himself according to his age and taste. This is both natural and essential. A child should put on children's clothes whereas teenagers will have clothes of their choice. They cannot interchange their dress. Humanity cannot be forced into adopting the culture of a particular era or country. Let humanity grow at its own pace. Let it expand and spread. For man loves variety and different experiences. Let us tap the universal and life-giving principles of religion and this will produce a new model. Let humanity be adorned with morals and manners. It will be then something fresh and long lasting. Also remember that whatever withers and decays should be discarded. We should not insist on retaining something that is rotten or obsolete.

Religion is the soul while culture is the form

Religion and culture follow different paths. Religion blesses us with the soul while culture is a form. Religion prescribes a way of life and code of conduct. It places certain restrictions and then lets man go about doing things. For example, a particular form of a pen may be specific to a culture. However,

---

[1] Nadwi, *Muslims in India*, 67-8.

religion is not at all concerned with any variety of a pen. It nonetheless demands that whenever pen is used, it should be for the cause of truth. Pen should promote goodness. Thus, religion provides us with the purpose of life and invests life with the soul. It monitors man's life yet it does not obstruct man's growth and evolution. The revival of any culture does not ensure man's salvation. This is true of every religious community, Hindus, Muslims and Christians alike.

Script or Conscience and Morals

Today, national language is a controversial issue, including a debate on its script. It appears as if it is an important issue for humanity or essential for the reform of the country. It was not the way of the Messengers of Allah. Script was not their concern. They were interested in the quality and outcome of writing. They insisted that one who writes should be truthful, God-conscious, honest and dutiful. His script is not important. In my speech in Benaras, I had raised the same point. If a document is forged, it is immaterial if it is written in Hindi or Urdu. It will remain a fake one, irrespective of its script. By the same token, a genuine document will be admissible, no matter which language or script. Messengers do not waste time and energy on the issue of a script issued. They rather train the hand of the writer in truth and honesty. They purify the heart and mind in a way that one writes only what is good and useful.

Messengers direct us to goals

It is not the job of Messengers to invent or discover things or produce gadgets. Rather, they produce such human beings who may use all resources for a good cause. Europe is good at producing resources. In contrast, Messengers guide us to the goals of life. True, Messengers did not create any machine but they transformed human beings. Europe has manufactured a variety of machines. The big question is who is to use these machines? Is it man with animal instincts? Today the crisis is that we have numerous resources, inventions and materials. But we do not have such human beings who may use them properly.

Humanity needs sympathetic human beings

Today humanity needs all of this: faith, conviction, truthfulness, piety, love, concern and sympathy for fellow human beings. Culture or script

Higher Moral Values

cannot solve the problems of humanity[2]. We stand in need of such human beings who are helpful, sympathetic, sensitive and self-sacrificing. Humanity is not generated by culture or script. Europe has robbed us of our morals and spiritual values. Since it did not have any spirituality, it deprived us of the same. We are now inundated with trivia and artificial, cosmetic items. We now lead a life full of glitter while we need inner, spiritual light. In the past we enjoyed spiritual happiness. Were we given a choice, which era would we opt for? Of course, we love to have an era of human values, mutual sympathy and love for fellow human beings. Today there is no respect and concern for humanity. We no doubt have printing press, electric light (and other conveniences) yet we lack the peace of mind. Now we rake in money and other material possessions but we are without spiritual values. We have worldly resources but do not know the purpose of life. For a thirsty person, water is most precious. He would have no interest in gold coins. In essence, our culture is devoid of mutual love, self-sacrifice and sympathy. Everyone is engrossed in his selfish desires. Such culture is worthless.

Loss of Spirituality

We have lost the way and do not have access to the straight way. We have blocked our heart and spirituality. With our selfish outlook we cannot attain spirituality. The heart is affected by worldliness, pride, and base desires. Our hearts do not affirm the authority of Allah. We do not believe in His might and glory. We do not hold ourselves accountable to Him. Given this, we face the present malaise. Owing to Godlessness we do not help one another. Nor do we risk our lives for others. Even real brothers consider each other as customers and business party. Exploitation is rife everywhere. The human nature has been corrupted. Parents are critical of their children and teachers are unhappy with their students[3].

Defective Educational System

There is outrage in universities these days that students do not respect their teachers whereas teachers do not have any concern or affection for students. It is worrisome for everyone. All sorts of efforts are being made to overcome the problem. However, no attention is paid to the root cause of this

---

[2] See Nadwi's perceptive comments on this issue in *Calamity of Linguistic and Cultural Chauvinism* (Lucknow, 1972).

[3] Nadwi, *Islam: An Introduction* (Lucknow, 1998), 152.

problem. Our educational system is basically materialistic[4]. So it breeds this problem. At no stage students are imparted moral training. The evil consequences are natural. Our literature and arts whet base desires, and encourage opportunism. Our whole social fabric is such that people are engaged only in gratifying their base desires. Our educational system prompts students to turn rich overnight. So there is a pressing need to change our outlook. Without transforming this, there can be no improvement.

Change in Mindset is Essential

We appreciate some of the reform and social movements in our country. If resources allow, we will co-operate with them. An instance in point is the Bhoodan movement. It is my considered opinion that before taking land, this message should be instilled that no one should have more land. People should voluntarily give land. Our outlook should be such that we should rejoice in giving out to the needy.

It is on record that there had been a feud between the inhabitants of Makkah and Madinah. Their culture and social norms were different. The Makkan believers were forced into migrating to Madinah. They had to leave behind all that they had in Makkah and arrived empty handed in Madinah. They were made brethren-in-faith of the rich Madinans. The latter welcomed them warmly. They placed before the Makkan migrants half of their assets, though they had no ties of kinship with them. The Makkans thanked and prayed for them. They were trained in a way that they sought only a small loan and some guidance about market. They were traders in Makkah and carried out the same in Madinah. The Prophet of Islam instilled self-sacrifice and sympathy into Madinans and self-esteem and self-respect into Makkans. As a result, the latter did not pay any attention to the wealth offered to them. They worked hard and earned money[5]. As we survey the scene of the present day migration among Muslims in general, we feel deeply dismayed. There is no sense of sacrifice, sympathy, self-confidence and self-respect among anyone.

We therefore insist on a change in the mindset. Let us develop such love for others that we share their sorrow. We should be so considerate as not to be indifferent to anyone's plight. Communism deploys state machinery for enforcing its policies. In contrast, religion changes the heart in a way that people disregard wealth. Once Prophet Muhammad (peace be upon

---

[4] Nadwi, *Western Civilisation, Islam and Muslims* (Lucknow, 1974), 167.

[5] Nadwi, *Muhammad, The Last Prophet*, 69.

him) rose to say prayer. He used to say that the coolness of his eyes is in his prayer. He would ask Bilal to make the call to prayer which would comfort and console him. On that day as he stood to pray, he abruptly left for home and then prayed. On being asked about his urgent work at home which had forced him to defer even prayer, he replied that he had left for home to direct his wife to give in charity some gold which he recalled was lying in his house.

No language is alien

I urge Muslims to keep their morale high. They should not have hatred for any language. As they once adopted Persian, they should opt for Hindi now. It is our indigenous language. I would nonetheless tell my Hindu brethren that they should reflect objectively on the whole issue. Mankind will not benefit from using this or that language. No particular culture can help humanity either. We all should develop the ideals of self- sacrifice, piety, values and respect for humanity. Today our conscience is off the right track. We are used to observing corruption in our public life. The Whites at one period used to think that human beings do not exist beyond the Atlantic Ocean. Likewise, people of one country do not consider those of another country as their equal. There is groupism everywhere, reeking of sheer selfishness.

The Russian Communists are after the interests of only one class while the American Capitalists favour another class[6]. They neglect classes and groups other than their own. For Russians only the working class matters while for Capitalists only the rich are worth considering. Such narrow nationalism or groupism is hazardous.

Need for God-conscious movement

Today there is a need for God-consciousness and love for humanity. A vigorous campaign is needed for this. It should be on a massive scale which should deal a fatal blow to selfishness, and base desires. This message should reach every nook and corner of the world that animal-like existence is not desirable. Materialism is rotten to the core. Selfishness has enervated the world. Man should recognise his worth and become alive to reality. People should forge their bond with Almighty Allah.

---

[6] Nadwi, *Islam and the World,* 137.

Need for an amalgam of knowledge and morals

We do not stand for ascetism and monasticism. We are not for retiring from this world to some cave. Rather, our call is for such spirituality which is aligned with this world. Our spirituality guides us in our life. We are not regressive. Nor do we believe in extremism. It is essential for humanity that morals, knowledge, science and God-consciousness should be blended. Today there is an extreme imbalance between these. There is no co-operation amid these. Science and morals have been moving in the two opposite directions.

Materialism and Asceticism

Materialism and asceticism today represent two ends of a scale[7]. Materialism is all about worldliness and worship of money. At the other end, asceticism renounces and detests life.

Our stance is that life should be taken as a gift of Allah which should be led in accordance with His directives. We should not be enslaved by worldliness. Rather, we should use the world as much as we need it. Life should be neither worshipped nor avoided. We must consider ourselves answerable to Allah. We must have the conviction that we will stand in His court and get divine recompense. We must repose trust in the altruistic, sincere Messengers of Allah. We should derive our way of life from them. We must devote ourselves to Allah. This is how we will be able to conquer the world.

---

[7] Ibid., 136.

The Present Malaise of the World

Disappointing Experience

Divisions mar the world presently. At an earlier date, ethnic groups and empires had divided countries. Now political issues have fragmented communities even at the local level. There was not so much menace under the pretext of religion, as is witnessed in today's civilised world which boasts of democracy. Today all political platforms are engaged in divisive politics and for increasing their clout. However, if people are called, they will respond. We do hope that people will assemble on a platform other than a political one. We urge people to reflect on human issues. It is gratifying that you have greeted our call. It is not surprising to note your revulsion towards divisive political issues. One learns from one's experience. We infer conclusions from regular happenings. Generally, people are assembled for vested interests. Please do trust us. We are not the mouthpiece of any political party. We are concerned with purely humanitarian issues.

Desire for control

Presently people ignore the degeneration around them. They appear complacent and are more interested in gaining their control over everything. They are after power. They do not mind immorality, bad manners, black marketing and lust for grabbing wealth. What concerns them most is their own trusteeship. Everyone wants to be in charge of things. As someone gains power, he maintains the status quo, and makes only nominal changes. As a result, degeneration goes unabated. There is not much divergence of opinion among various political parties about the causes of disorder. They do not condemn the all-round degeneration. Their only contention is that they should enjoy power. They have no problem with the rotten system. Their main objective is how to retain their control over the system.

The Scenario in Europe and Asia

The same motives were behind all the major wars in the world. France, England, Germany, Russia and US were inspired by the same motives. While resorting to propaganda they sought to have control over colonies. They were opposed to other colonisers while they themselves wanted to be the coloniser. Any humanitarian issues did not evoke their attention. They were not keen on preaching Prophet Jesus's faith. Nor did they try to establish justice on earth or eliminate indecency, injustice and oppression. This was the attitude of all, be they the English, Germans, Russians or Americans. Truth or falsehood, and injustice and fairness were not their concern. They never thought of blessing the world with a decent way of life and of serving fellow human beings. Their only interest was to grab the wealth of the colonies under their control[1]. They wanted to make most of the natural resources of the countries under their control. They wanted to have their monopoly over the world. Their only way of life was to exploit others for grabbing wealth. Their national glory consisted in destroying fellow human beings. They were swayed by their base desires, especially greed and lust, as they were after only wealth. They did not refrain from drinking and gambling. They were utterly Godless people who acted against their essential human nature. They were devoid of kindness and mercy and had no interest in humanity. Our own countrymen, castes, clans, political parties and national institutions and nationalist governments have been following in the same footsteps. They want themselves and their coterie to enjoy life and thus they accept the present situation. They have differences with only those who are in power. They are not interested in transforming the world. They are after only a change in leadership. They want to take others' place. You all are a witness to elections for District Board, Municipality and Town Area, etc. New candidates contest these elections. But does any of them present before you a new vision, a new outlook, a new way of life, a new strategy for serving humanity and a new plan for reform? Has any new Board or Committee ever been successful in stemming moral disorder? Does anyone serve humanity selflessly? What we have experienced all along is that all of them share the same traits, same way of life and same outlook. As a result, there is no change in our condition. All ailments and problems persist.

---

[1] Nadwi, *Muslims in The West*, 28-29.

The Present Malaise of the World

Messengers of Allah identify ailments

In contrast, the Messengers of Allah plainly point to the flawed lifestyle. They urge people to change their mindset altogether. It is akin to an ill-fitting dress. Nominal alterations cannot do any good. As long as basic problems are not addressed, there will be trouble. That is why they ask people to adopt a new way of life.

People are deluded

Today we consider ourselves free in gratifying our desires. Far from campaigning against base desires, all political parties encourage people to fulfil their desires, without any regard for morals. They promise people that once they are in power, they will let people do whatever they want. They will let them enjoy life to the brim. With such tall promises they seek their vote and support. Every political party insists that it will let people lead a life of comfort and luxury. It is like spoiling a child by offering him sweets. They thus mislead people. They treat people like children and fan their desires. They are bent on spoiling their habits and mindset. Man is liable to ask for more and more, no matter how much he may get. Cinema has made man more demanding and excitable. For movies add to his excitement. People would love to have more and more nudity on screen. Thus, there is no check and balance on man's desires. Rather, the leaders whet their appetite for more[2].

This is not the way of the Messengers of Allah. They strike a balance in man's desires. They insist that it is unnatural to gratify each and every desire. They discourage man's greed and take steps to control it. So doing, they do not care about people's resentment. They face protest and opposition. Regardless of the challenges they face, they know that man should learn self-restraint and follow the straight way. Checking greed and base desires is essential. There is no point in expressing dismay and shock over the evil consequences of unbridled desires.

An Unbridled Race

Political parties have a flawed system in accepting the present order. They see uncontrolled forces trampling and devastating humanity. Yet these parties

---

[2] Nadwi, *Guidance From the Holy Qur'cn*, 219-20.

are a slave to such forces. There is a race of unbridled forces, without any regard for conscience, morals and sympathy for fellow human beings. Europe and US pay a lip service to equality and sympathy. However, their track record is well known. Under the guise of sympathy, they seek to establish their hegemony. They resort to unthinkable forms of injustice and exploitation.

Who is fit to rule and hold a position?

We are of the firm view that we have lost the way. Until we develop conviction in Allah, there can be no reform. Without this we cannot transform wrongdoers. My assertion is not some random thought. I have reached this conclusion in the light of my thorough study. We cannot reach the model of humanity unless we have God-consciousness. Let us disgorge our mind of lust for high positions and wealth. Let us develop self-sacrifice and concern for others. Prophet Muhammad (peace be upon him) is on record advising that only such be given a position who do not hanker after it. He laid down this unique qualification. In stark contrast, today we brazenly indulge in self-praise for grabbing power. The Prophet's Companions shied away from assuming any post. 'Umar pleaded that he be relieved of the burden of a public office. He was, however, forced into accepting his post. As long as he held office, he did his job conscientiously. He felt much relieved after performing his duty. Khalid ibn Walid was appointed commander-in-chief. Everyone held him in awe. In the midst of the battle he was stripped of his position and was replaced by Abu Ubaydah. This did not grieve him at all. Graciously he remarked: "As I performed this duty as an act of worship, I will continue doing so. However, if I did only for the sake of 'Umar, I will stop fighting."[3] It was observed that he participated in all later battles with the same fervour. His dismissal did not have any effect on his attitude.

Greed for Political Power

Today if someone is expelled from a political party, he avoids it or creates mischief. Even if he departs, he sets up his own political party. For he is after only a high position, honour and glory. Unless we change our mindset, there cannot be any reform. I tell you these realities of life without mincing

---

[3] Nadwi, *Muslims in the West*, 146.

words. Let us develop the fear of Allah and seek to win His pleasure. Let us transform ourselves morally and spiritually. Let us abandon the false ideal of enjoying life.

Man's basic needs are limited

The list of man's basic needs is not very long. Of course, the list of luxuries is endless. We all hanker after luxuries. People's objects of desire are comfort, good food and base self. People do not believe in Allah. Rather, they reject His majesty. Man is taken as an evolved, developed animal and it is believed that he should be free to gratify all of his desires. Because of all this there is so much chaos and degeneration. Until we change this mindset, all efforts for reform will remain fruitless. Even a small municipality will not be reformed, what to talk of a town or a country.

Rotten units cannot make up a good product

Today individuals and components of society are corrupted. Their very foundation is flawed. People have been brought up in unhealthy atmosphere. As a result, all human institutions are faulty and weak. Organisations are made up of individuals.

Unless individuals turn pious, their organisations cannot work well. Whenever the issue of individuals is raised, there is much resentment. It angers people and they want to avoid this issue. They have this false notion that no wrong will mar collective life. Let me use an analogy. It is like as if one examines bricks of a kiln and finds them of poor quality, unfit to be used in a building and yet one insists that once a structure is raised, everything will be all right. How can something defective result in a good product? Wicked members cannot constitute a good, decent organisation. Rotten logs of wood cannot help build a quality boat. Our observation is that all units and material are defective. Naturally, it will not lead to a good structure. We cannot have an efficient, honest Municipality and District Board with men of no integrity. Likewise, we cannot have a government which may not deliver the goods. This is the present scenario. No one is worried about the material used while he resents ugly results. Is this not foolish on our part? Messengers of Allah build character and transform individuals into righteous human beings. Their groundwork is stable and substantial. They do not cheat. Our reality: truth is disregarded even in our educational institutions. No effort is made for developing morals and conviction. There is no arrangement for moral upbringing. There are untrained people everywhere. Students are also not imparted any useful training. It is common knowledge what kind of people are at the helm of affairs at Municipality, District Board and government. They call the shots. They are human beings only in name.

Manifest Truth

Truth eventually manifests itself, no matter how much it is suppressed. A donkey in a tiger's skin cannot fool others. Many of you are very keen about reform. Have you ever tried to do some cleansing at a lower level? People are only after political power. What needs to be done is to have respect for humanity and fear of Allah.

Commercialisation

Human habitations are treated as market place. Everyone takes others as consumers. This commercialisation is destructive. Everyone is concerned about his rights and privileges. There is a conflict everywhere: between students and teachers, and between workers and factory owners. Why is there a class war? This is a manifestation of our mercenary nature. The Messengers of Allah instruct us in discharging our obligations to others. They remind us of our duties. We should be particular about fulfilling our duty and generous about our rights. With this change in heart there will be a marked change in atmosphere. We will be then able to enjoy life. However, today exploitation is rife and our outlook is purely mercenary. We do not care about helpless human beings[4].

Our Message

We believe our message is relevant for every party. We are more important than any party. For if we succeed, humanity will blossom. It will put an end to man's present plight. Today few care about humanity. Our message is to revive and reinforce human values. Let us all work for humanity. Let us strive to produce role models. We are not here to obstruct anyone. Our message is that we should be concerned about humanity. Our worry is the present degeneration. This was the mission of the Messengers of Allah. We want to remind you all of the same concern. People are lost in their restricted roles, concerned at most about material issues. Religion blesses

---

[4] Nadwi, *Islamic Concept of Prophethood*, 116-8.

The Present Malaise of the World

us with conviction and love for Allah; it invests us with the peace of mind. The Messengers' hard work led to mankind's happiness. Instead, men are culprits of this gross negligence. While forgetting their real asset, they have turned into agents of worthless capitalists. They have turned mercenary in their outlook. It was not their role and mandate. Their task was to preach and promote faith. However, they lost their way. Had they championed their mission and love for human beings, they would have been blessed with honour and success. They should reclaim their position and it would ensure success for them. Mankind would do well to appreciate the Messengers' teachings. Political parties and groups should give up their tussle for power and monopoly. They should redress the present degeneration. They should not think only of themselves, their near and dear ones and their friends. Rather, they should have concern for the entire humanity. For without such reform no one can enjoy peace and happiness.

Dedication

Two influential figures who have been responsible for the multivolume project on Shaykh Nadwi's life and legacy have sadly passed on. This has been a great loss for the Ahsan Academy of Research. Dr Yusuf Bamjee (d. 2020), was instrumental in setting up the Academy in 2017 to promote the works of Shaykh Nadwi and other pioneering scholars in the field of *tajdīd* (Islamic resurgence). The following comment is reproduced here to highlight his pro-active role to the Shaykh Nadwi series:

"I am very much obliged to my colleague, Dr Yusuf Bamjee whose support in every possible way has motivated me to study Islamic scholarship in South Asia. He has given me valuable feedback and encouragement at every stage of the writing process. The multivolume publication of which the present study forms one volume owes its inception to Yusuf. His discerning interest, keen eye for technical production and standards of excellence are reflective of his work ethic and generosity."

Sadly, I have to use the past tense to express my enormous sense of gratitude to the late Mufti Ayoob Moola (d. 2019). A mentor and friend, Mufti Ayoob was always a source of inspiration. His deep interest in the progress of the study and the special duā's for its successful completion are things I now cherish most. This work, in more than one way, is a tribute to his blessed memory.

30 August 2023
Abdul Kader Choughley